CHRISTCHURCH
CRIMES
1850–75

CHRISTCHURCH CRIMES
1850–75

SCANDAL & SKULDUGGERY IN PORT & TOWN

Geoffrey W. Rice

CANTERBURY UNIVERSITY PRESS

UNIVERSITY OF
CANTERBURY
Te Whare Wananga o Waitaha
CHRISTCHURCH NEW ZEALAND

First published in 2012 by
CANTERBURY UNIVERSITY PRESS
University of Canterbury
Private Bag 4800, Christchurch
NEW ZEALAND
www.cup.canterbury.ac.nz

ISBN 978-1-927145-39-5

A catalogue record for this book is available from the
National Library of New Zealand.

Cover cartoon by John Leech, in *Punch*, vol. 18 (1850), p. 240.
Evangelical politicians had proposed a ban on all work on the
Sabbath, and *Punch* wondered if this would also apply to the police.
Hence the poster, 'The Police have strict orders NOT to take any
person into custody on Sunday'. People may walk to church, but
otherwise 'the streets would be exclusively occupied by thieves, with
nobody to rob but one another'.

Design and layout by Quentin Wilson, Christchurch
Printed by PrintStop, Wellington

CONTENTS

ACKNOWLEDGEMENTS

I wish to thank Professor Jeremy Finn for his articles on the courts in early Canterbury, Colin Amodeo for his research on the establishment of Lyttelton and early Christchurch, the late Madeleine Seager for her biography of her grandfather, and David Gee for his pioneering history of the Lyttelton Gaol, all of which were particularly valuable resources for the writing of this book.

Finally, as always, my warm thanks to the team at Canterbury University Press for spotting my mistakes and smoothing the path to publication: Rachel Scott, publisher; Anna Rogers, editor; and Quentin Wilson, designer.

PREFACE

This is a collection of stories based on newspaper reports of civil and criminal cases heard in the Christchurch and Lyttelton courts in the first quarter-century of the Canterbury settlement. It is not an academic study, and has very few endnotes, but the sources for each chapter are easily identified as the newspapers of the day. Nor is it a work of fiction: the events here described actually happened. Rather it should be regarded as an attempt at evidence-based reconstruction of crimes and courtroom proceedings, opening a window on the lives and deeds of ordinary people who lived in this place over 140 years ago.

Readers in need of further background or context may wish to consult my previous books, *Christchurch Changing: An illustrated history* (Canterbury University Press, 2nd edn, 2008), and *Lyttelton: Port and Town* (Canterbury University Press, 2005), which attempt to explain in simple narrative the founding and growth of New Zealand's second-largest city and its port.

Readers who just want to enjoy the stories – often dramatic and even sensational, sometimes horrifying, sometimes amusing, frequently rather sad – may skip straight to the first chapter, but some of you may want to know how this book came into being, and why it has been written.

Over the past few years I have been working on a book about Christchurch's Market Place, which was renamed Victoria Square in 1903. The western side of the square comprised the city's legal precinct, dominated in the late nineteenth century by a splendid Gothic-style Supreme Court and a modest Magistrate's Court. In 1989 the Supreme Court was replaced by a modern Law Courts building, now partially screened from the square by the large willow trees lining the Avon River. In order to understand what went on in the western part of the Market Place, I set myself the task of reading the court reports in the city's daily newspapers, the *Press* from 1862, the older *Lyttelton Times* and the latter's evening edition, the *Star*.

This became an absorbing and fascinating part of my research, yet I knew that only a handful of these cases could be included in a book about Victoria Square. Apart from a few crimes committed in the square, and a near-riot following one sensational murder trial, most cases had nothing to do with the square. As the pile of research notes mounted, however, it occurred to me that there was more than enough material for another book. I had found so many gripping stories buried in these court reports that I felt sure other people, too, would find them interesting.

Then came the Christchurch earthquakes of September 2010 and February 2011. Archives New Zealand, the Canterbury Museum, the central city library and the city council's archives were all closed indefinitely, and the last remains closed as I write these words. My work on Victoria Square came to a sudden halt. More than half the book was written, but I needed access to the city council archives in order to finish the story of the square's transformation in the 1980s.

Having recently retired from the University of Canterbury, after nearly 40 years as an academic historian, I had the unaccustomed luxury of time on my hands. Some of that was reserved for my family, especially a new grandson, and some was swallowed up by another book documenting Christchurch's lost chimney heritage (*All Fall Down*, Canterbury University Press, 2011), but once this was finished

I decided to write about Christchurch's early crimes and scandals. Why? Because I found them intensely interesting.

As a historian I have always had a lively curiosity about human behaviour, and what motivates people to step outside their normal boundaries. For many years I taught a course on the French Revolution, and one of the fascinations of that subject is trying to figure out why otherwise peaceful and respectable people were willing to break the law and even kill each other for the sake of abstract ideas. As the novelist C. P. Snow once remarked, civilisation is but a thin coat of varnish, and the beast lurks within all of us. It is terribly easy for law and order to break down, as we saw during the urban riots across Britain and Europe in 2011.

History is usually written by the winners, according to a popular axiom, and the bulk of the evidence used by historians has been produced by literate social elites, institutions or government departments. It is rare to hear the voices of ordinary folk from the remote past. Even the nineteenth century is now getting increasingly remote from our present age of the internet, Facebook and Twitter. Most ordinary people back then were too busy, or too tired, or insufficiently literate, to write letters or keep diaries. Even today most people live in the present moment, with scarcely a thought for the past, which is why so many people are condemned, as Santayana warned us, to repeat their mistakes.

Yet such were the shorthand skills of nineteenth-century newspaper reporters that courtroom testimony and cross-examinations were often captured verbatim, especially in the more sensational murder trials. Reading these reports one can almost hear the voices of the past. We catch glimpses of cabbies, shopkeepers, clerks and housewives going about their daily work, with descriptions of homes or workplaces, and the occasional fight in a pub. What the printed record cannot show, however, are their accents, dialects, gestures or facial expressions. On the streets of Victorian Christchurch one could hear the regional accents of almost every part of the British Isles. Sydenham, 'the model borough' and quintessential working-class suburb of old Christchurch, was once known as 'Lanky-Town' after a shipload of migrants from Lancashire settled there.

Whatever the accent, not all of this testimony can be taken at face value. Respectable witnesses were probably telling the truth as they saw it, but desperate and frightened people, even under oath, will lie and conceal the truth. The jury is there to assess the credibility of each witness, and to decide on guilt or innocence. In most cases, these juries reached their decisions remarkably quickly, sometimes even without retiring. In some of the cases described in these pages, the jury ignored clear directions from the judge, and acquitted or convicted for reasons that remain obscure to us. Yet the jury was then, and still is, assumed to reflect the views of society at large.

It may be objected that a collection of crimes and scandals will tend to give a distorted impression of Canterbury society over a century ago. This is perfectly true. The great bulk of the population was never in trouble with the police and never appeared in court. Such deep stigma was attached to anyone who had served time in prison that respectable people avoided any contact with known criminals. As Benjamin Franklin once observed, it takes many good deeds to build a good reputation, and only one bad one to lose it. Most people believed that honesty was the best policy, and managed to behave themselves throughout their lives, but not everyone behaves entirely virtuously in any age. Some of society's shrewdest wrongdoers have never been found out or brought before a judge.

This book is about the ones who got caught, and were called to account. Their crimes mirror the realities of colonial life in Canterbury and range across a wide variety of charges, from simple theft of a watch (or a blanket or a box of soap), stealing sheep or a horse, shooting a cow, drunkenness, disturbing the peace, forging a signature on a stolen cheque, setting fire to a haystack or a hotel, defrauding a partner or embezzling an employer, failing to pay a debt, deserting a wife or committing bigamy, wilful damage to property, selling sheep infected with scab, purveying alcohol outside the licensed hours or keeping a brothel, to the more serious criminal matters of rape, assault with intent to inflict grievous bodily harm, stabbing, poisoning, manslaughter and murder.

Some people may regard a book like this as mere muck-raking in the past, a collection of salacious stories for the prurient. In fact most nineteenth-century newspapers refused to publish details about sexual offending, especially what were then regarded as 'unnatural acts', often with the simple disclaimer, 'the facts were not fit for publication'. Adultery and fornication were fair game, however, and one of the strongest motives for most people to behave themselves was the fear of being shamed by having one's name and crime reported in the newspapers.

There are plenty of moral lessons in the following pages, for those who like to stand in judgement, or want to learn from the mistakes of others. Perhaps the strongest impression one gains from reading nineteenth-century court reports is of the role played by alcohol in so much criminal behaviour. It was common for men accused of stupid or violent acts to mutter that they were drunk at the time and therefore somehow not responsible for their actions. One of the saddest cases is that of the mother accused of causing the death of her new-born baby. Her eldest son, 'only a little boy', told the court that she had been drunk on whisky for a week before the baby's death. He had been sent out to buy it. There are many stories here about individuals who made wrong decisions or poor choices without thinking of the likely consequences. Some were so desperate for cash that they risked imprisonment and social ruin for quite small sums of money.

Judges were sometimes criticised for imposing heavier sentences for fraud or embezzlement than for crimes against the person, such was the colossal respect for property and money in the nineteenth century. Such crimes were regarded not simply as theft, but as breaches of the trust placed in employees or business partners, and therefore striking at the very foundations of civil society. This book will tend to give a lopsided view of crime in Canterbury because it concentrates on crimes against the person, yet the bulk of cases heard in the province were about money. The Magistrate's Court dealt with a large number of actions for debt, but these were rarely reported in detail. In August 1866 the *Press* made a typical remark:

'There were only a large number of debt cases disposed of today, but none of any interest whatever to the public.' Cases of fraud or embezzlement were often long and complex, and are difficult to summarise briefly, or interestingly. They are also of little interest to legal historians, unless they involve some unusual point of law.

For some readers there may be a few surprises in the following pages, for the New Zealand legal system as it operated in the nineteenth century was not exactly the same as the one we now enjoy. Punishments were much harsher back then, with imprisonment nearly always accompanied by hard labour, when troublesome prisoners were shackled in leg-irons to slow them down. New Zealand in the 1850s was still close to the era of transportation of British convicts to the Australian penal colonies. For crimes of a sexual nature, held to outrage moral standards, judges could still impose a whipping, with 12 and occasionally 24 strokes of the lash added to a prison sentence.

Some of the high-profile cases from this period have already been described in previous publications such as David Gee, *The Devil's Own Brigade: A history of the Lyttelton Gaol, 1860–1920* (Millwood Press, Wellington, 1975); or *Sharing the Challenge* (J. C. Rowe and Christchurch Police History Book Committee, 1989), a social and pictorial history of the Christchurch Police District by Barry Thomson and Robert Neilson, but are worth retelling for a new generation. Richard S. Hill's monumental early volumes of the official New Zealand Police history, *Policing the Colonial Frontier* and *The Colonial Frontier Tamed* (Government Print, Wellington, 1986 and 1989), occasionally touch on Christchurch crimes, while *Portrait of a Profession: The centennial book of the New Zealand Law Society* (A. H. & A. W. Reed, Wellington, 1969), edited by Robin Cooke QC (later Lord Cooke), provides much useful information about Canterbury's early judges and lawyers.

Fortunately for those who seek scholarly analysis of Canterbury court cases in the nineteenth century, Professor Jeremy Finn of the School of Law at the University of Canterbury has published several excellent articles that provide a contextual framework for the stories recounted in this book, most notably 'Debt, drunkenness and desertion: The Resident Magistrate's Court in early Canterbury, 1851–61', *New Zealand Universities Law Review*, 21:3 (June 2005), 452–85, and ' "Not having the fear of God before her eyes": Enforcement of the criminal law in the Supreme Court in Canterbury, 1852–1872', *Canterbury Law Review*, 11 (2005), 250–82.

Other books that I have found useful and readers may enjoy include Colin Amodeo's *Forgotten Forty-Niners: Being an account of the men & women who paved the way in 1849 for the Canterbury Pilgrims in 1850* (Caxton Press, Christchurch, 2003); the essay collection *Remembering Godley: A portrait of Canterbury's founder* (Hazard Press, Christchurch, 2001), edited by Mark Stocker; *Poison: The coward's weapon* by David Gee (Whitcoulls, Christchurch, 1985); *College! A history of Christ's College* by Don Hamilton (Christ's College Board of Governors, Christchurch, 1996); Gordon Ogilvie's *Ballantynes: The story of Dunstable House, 1854–2004* (J. Ballantyne & Co., Christchurch, 2004); *A Woman of Good Character: Single women as immigrant settlers in nineteenth-century New Zealand* by Charlotte Macdonald (Bridget Williams Books, Wellington, 1990); Sherwood Young's *Guilty on the Gallows: Famous capital crimes of New Zealand* (Grantham House, Wellington, 1999); *'Ready Money': The life of William Robinson of Hill River, South Australia, and Cheviot Hills, North Canterbury* by Margaret Wigley (Canterbury University Press, Christchurch, 2006); and Charles A. L. Treadwell's *Notable New Zealand Trials* (Thomas Avery, New Plymouth, 1936).

I have given metric equivalents in the text for measurements but monetary comparisons must be less precise. Using the Reserve Bank's New Zealand inflation calculator (www.rbnz.govt.nz), we can estimate that £50 in the 1850s would now be worth about $5000, so some of the fines and sureties set by judges and magistrates were challenging for people who were often unemployed or only modestly paid.

Newspaper reports of cases in the Magistrate's Court are usually very brief, but a few further details can sometimes be gleaned from police records and the court minute books. The Christchurch office of Archives New Zealand has minute books of court proceedings from 1852 onwards, and trial files for the Supreme Court from 1855.

The 'Return of Prisoners Tried or Committed for Sentence from 1852 to 1897' is open to public scrutiny. By contrast, Supreme Court cases, especially those that aroused public interest, were often very fully reported in the newspapers.

This book was made possible by the newspaper digitisation project of the National Library of New Zealand. While the university and public libraries were closed for long periods after the Christchurch earthquakes, and their microfilm of the major Christchurch newspapers remained inaccessible, early issues of the *Lyttelton Times* 1851–62 and the *Star* from 1868 to 1909 were available online from *Papers Past*. I have relied mainly on the *Star* for cases after 1868. After the book was completed, the first 50 years of the *Press* also became available. While its court reports are usually very similar to those of the *Star* and *Lyttelton Times*, the *Press* occasionally provides different details. Unlike microfilm, which is hard on the eyes and clumsy to use, *Papers Past* enables keyword searching. For the historian, the digital age has been a great blessing, making an increasing range of primary sources available online.

The Canterbury Settlement

T he city of Christchurch, founded in 1850 and now New Zealand's second-largest city, was planned as the capital of the Canterbury settlement, the last and most successful of a series of British colonising projects in Australia and New Zealand set up according to the theories of Edward Gibbon Wakefield, a convicted child abductor and visionary politician. His colonisation ideas were much discussed in early nineteenth-century England as a means of easing overpopulation and crowding in rapidly growing industrial cities. Instead of the earlier convict colonies of Australia or the lawless frontiers of previous European settlements in the Americas, Wakefield envisaged a process of 'systematic colonisation'. In simple terms, his idea was to set a high price for land, a 'sufficient price' that would generate funds for schools and churches and enable what he hoped would be 'instant civilisation'. His aim was to transplant what one colonist called 'a slice of Old England, cut from top to bottom', with a landowning gentry, farmers, labourers, merchants and artisans in a compact agricultural settlement. Wakefield founded a Colonisation Society to promote his ideas, and in 1834 the British Parliament gave its approval to found a settlement in South Australia, with its capital to be named Adelaide, after Queen Adelaide, consort of William IV.

Wakefield then formed an association to promote 'systematic colonisation' in New Zealand, but he rejected the government's terms for a royal charter. He then went to Canada and, in his absence, the New Zealand Association was reformed as a joint stock company, the New Zealand Company. In 1839 Wakefield's brother William sailed to set up its first settlement in the North Island, to be named Wellington after the victor of the Battle of Waterloo. There was, however, insufficient land for the arriving settlers, and an overflow settlement was established at Whanganui (first known as Petre). New Plymouth was then established in 1841. Wakefield's younger brother Arthur led the Nelson settlement in 1842, but was killed in the Wairau Incident in 1843. The Free Church of Scotland then began to plan a South Island settlement, according to Wakefield's plan, and its agent chose Otago Harbour as the site for its capital, to be named Dunedin. The first shipload of settlers arrived there in March 1848.

The Treaty of Waitangi, signed in February 1840, had secured British sovereignty over New Zealand, and brought the indigenous Maori population under the protective blanket of British law. Unfortunately, the Maori version of the treaty included concepts that were different from the accepted English notion of sovereignty, and many Maori believed they had retained both ownership and control of their ancestral lands. These misunderstandings would lead to war in the North Island in the 1860s, but in the meantime large amounts of land were purchased from the Maori for British settlers and their families.

Canterbury was planned as an Anglican settlement, with a bishop and plenty of clergy to maintain a high moral tone. Lord Lyttelton headed the Canterbury Association, with an impressive committee including the Archbishop of Canterbury and titled investors. A young Anglo-Irish lawyer and landowner named John Robert Godley had devised a scheme to resettle Irish farmers in Canada after the potato famine, but Wakefield persuaded him to switch his scheme to New Zealand, and to lead the Canterbury settlement. Godley was a deeply religious man, with high connections in both church and government.

Captain Joseph Thomas, an experienced engineer who had already travelled widely in New Zealand, was appointed chief surveyor in May 1848 to select a site and start a survey. By then there were small numbers of Europeans scattered along the east coast of the South Island, including shore whalers and former convicts from Australia. New Zealand was never a penal colony, to which convicts were shipped, but some of the men and women who had served their time in Tasmania or New South Wales crossed the Tasman in search of a better life, and not a few escaped convicts on the run turned up under assumed names.

On the south side of Banks Peninsula a small French settlement had been established at Akaroa in 1840, just after the signing of the Treaty of Waitangi, and the first British magistrates for the South Island had arrived with Captain Owen Stanley aboard HMS *Britomart* on 11 August 1840. Charles Barrington Robinson was resident magistrate at Akaroa until 1846, but he had very little to do, as the French officials controlled their own people. His successor, John Watson, remained until 1870, and held the first court at Lyttelton in 1850, when the northern harbour was still called Port Cooper.

By the end of 1848 Captain Thomas had selected Port Cooper and the Canterbury Plains as the best site for the new settlement, and 1849 was taken up with land purchasing and surveying. Thomas originally intended placing the capital or chief town at the head of the harbour, but there was not enough flat land there, and in July 1849 he switched to an open grassy site surrounded by swamps on the coastal plain, east of a farm established at Putaringamotu (Riccarton) by the Deans brothers in 1843. (It is said that the size of their carrots convinced him that a settlement here could at least feed itself.) At Purau on the south side of Port Cooper the pioneering Rhodes brothers ran a thriving sheep farm, so the settlers also had a ready supply of fresh meat.

The capital was to be called Christchurch, after Godley's college at Oxford University. Port Cooper was renamed Port Victoria, and workmen were recruited in Wellington and Hobart to start building a jetty and accommodation for the hundreds of migrants who were about to be signed up by the Canterbury Association's energetic emigration agent, James Edward FitzGerald. As cottages began to appear among the surveyors' tents above Cavendish Bay during 1850, this 'little town' was renamed Lyttelton, after the association's chairman. Before long, Port Victoria was renamed Lyttelton Harbour. Thus the scene was set for the establishment of law and order in the Canterbury settlement.

CHAPTER ONE

GODLEY DEALS WITH THE UNGODLY

John Robert Godley
(1814–1861), lawyer, writer,
administrator, colonist,
magistrate and chief
agent of the Canterbury
Settlement, was later
assistant under-secretary
at the War Office in
London.

Cyclopedia of New Zealand,
vol. 3, Canterbury, 1903

J ohn Robert Godley was Christchurch's first resident magistrate. The base of his statue in Cathedral Square bears the simple inscription 'Founder of Canterbury', and the title is apt. Though many others had a hand in establishing the Canterbury settlement, Godley was its undoubted leader until his return to England in 1852. When he arrived at Lyttelton as the Canterbury Association's leader and official agent on 14 April 1850 he was astonished that so much had already been achieved. Besides the jetty, there were four immigration barracks and a cookhouse, and a substantial home for the Godleys. Enterprising merchants were setting up stores and grog-shops to serve the workmen and their families. But Captain Thomas had spent almost all of his budget, and the road that was to link the port to the capital on the plains had barely been begun. Godley returned to Wellington, where he pledged his own credit to raise funds to complete essential work, but in the meantime most of the workers had to be laid off.

According to Colin Amodeo's excellent account of early Lyttelton in *Forgotten Forty-Niners*, law enforcement was sorely needed in this primitive village of unemployed navvies and former convicts. Thomas had asked Akaroa's resident magistrate for two constables, and in May 1850 John Watson sent Peter Cameron and J. Sheed to Lyttelton, where they were housed first in a raupo hut, then in a cob cottage and finally in a room in one of the first hotels. Watson held court in Lyttelton every fortnight and, as might be expected in such a community, with occasional ships bringing timber and supplies, most of the charges were for drunkenness, assault and desertion.

Godley returned to Lyttelton early in December 1850, with his wife Charlotte and their little boy Arthur, as the first of the immigrant ships were expected that month, having left England early in September. With a growing population now at Lyttelton, 34-year-old Dr William Donald had been appointed by Governor George Grey as the port's medical officer. He arrived by the brig *Sisters* on 7 November, and was to become the port's leading citizen and later resident magistrate (1861–81). The Canterbury Association's solicitor, Christopher Edward Dampier, arrived next day by the *Phoebe Dunbar*. Dampier was to become the settlement's leading lawyer in the 1850s. The *Charlotte Jane* was the first immigrant ship to arrive, on the morning of 16 December 1850, with 154 passengers, including FitzGerald, followed that afternoon by the *Randolph* with 210 passengers. Next day the *Sir George Seymour* sailed into Lyttelton, with 227 passengers, and 10 days later the *Cressy* with 215 passengers. It was astonishing that the first three ships had arrived almost together after more than three months of solitary sailing around half the globe.

These were the famous 'First Four Ships' that started the Canterbury settlement, but many more vessels were chartered by the Canterbury Association: the *Castle Eden* and *Isabella Hercus* were the first of 15 other ships bringing settlers during 1851. Yet more migrants arrived from other parts of New Zealand, and from Australia, with capital and livestock. By the time Canterbury celebrated its first anniversary on 16 December 1851, 3000 people had settled on farms or in the two main towns. Lyttelton was the larger settlement and the centre of officialdom – with the association offices, the post office, the custom house, courtroom and lockup – until 1854, when Christchurch finally overtook it with a population of 924 in 183 houses. Confined by its steep-sided cove, Lyttelton remained a small port town, while Christchurch grew steadily to become the provincial capital, with over 16,000 residents by 1876.

Godley held his first court as resident magistrate on 20 December 1850, to deal with charges arising from the unhappy voyage of the *Randolph*. Captain William Dale was a strict disciplinarian, more accustomed to conveying convicts than migrants, and in November he had two seamen placed in irons when they refused to work. After the ship arrived at Lyttelton three crewmen went on strike, and one of them, John Russell, punched Dale on the mouth after quarrelling with a passenger. Second officer Samuel Sheard confirmed the captain's account and Russell was fined £2 (about $200 in today's money). Unable to pay the fine, he was sentenced to 14 days in the lockup. Two other sailors, John Cormick and James Reeve, were given seven days. The lockup was a flimsy wooden A-frame hut of the type perversely known among the Canterbury settlers as a V-hut.

As one of his neighbours wrote of him, 'Godley administered such ample justice as the present state of crime in Lyttelton required. That is not very appalling. Cases brought before him arise chiefly out of quarrels between seamen and captains of ships, assaults and small robberies committed by old hands.' Surveyor Charles Torlesse described Godley as 'very high-principled and conscientious', but also at times hasty and obstinate, which made him unpopular with some. Another settler, Conway Rose, observed that the little settlement was not large enough for someone of Godley's undoubted ability: 'he was like a whale in a duck-pond'. FitzGerald simply thought Godley was head and shoulders above any other man in early Canterbury in both character and talent.[1]

One of the steerage passengers from the *Sir George Seymour*, Eli Salt, suffered the stigma of being the first of the migrants to be convicted of a criminal offence. He appeared before Godley on 2 January 1851 charged with having stolen a door worth 5s, the property of the Canterbury Association. Eli was living in the barracks with his wife Hannah and their three boys while he worked as a 'lumper' (stevedore) on the jetty and built his first house in the gully that was known for many years as Salt's Gully and is now Hawkhurst Road. He had bought several doors from the association's storekeeper, Gustav Gartner – known as 'the Baron' and later publican of the Golden Fleece Hotel in Christchurch – but Gartner claimed that Salt had deliberately taken the wrong set of doors, with one more than he had paid for. Godley believed his official's testimony, and sent Salt to the lockup for seven days.

A seaman from the *Cressy*, Samuel Bishop, appeared before Godley on 3 January 1851 charged with desertion and unlawfully taking a ship's boat. Captain Bell, having recovered the boat, withdrew the charge of larceny, but Bishop was convicted of desertion and sentenced to a fortnight in the lockup. For the rest of that month the charges heard by Godley included assault, theft, breach of contract and drunkenness. In February 15 sailors from the newly arrived *Castle Eden* refused to work and were sentenced to 14 days' confinement on board with stoppage of wages.

Godley heard Canterbury's first smuggling case on 22 January 1851. George Armstrong, master of the cutter *Katherine Johnstone*, was charged with having five quarter-casks of contraband spirits and a hogshead of wine on board his vessel. Mr Ballard, the acting landing-waiter at Lyttelton, had searched the vessel at Sumner on 20 January and found the contraband. Armstrong said he had obtained the wine and spirits from a French whaler at Akaroa, but his manifest stated the vessel to be in ballast. The ballast had not been sufficient to cover the contraband. Armstrong said he was willing to pay the duty, and had gone ashore to get the money to do so. After questioning other witnesses, Godley concluded that an illegal unshipment from the French vessel had taken place, and the vessel and contraband goods were forfeited to the Crown. But Armstrong was allowed to repurchase his ship, and was soon back in the coastal trade. Perhaps Godley had regarded this solution as a suitable equivalent of a fine that did not deprive the man of his livelihood.

Godley was joined on the magistrate's bench in 1851 by two justices of the peace, sub-collector of customs Henry Godfrey Gouland, and lawyer Edward Ward, eldest son of the Honourable and Reverend Henry Ward of Killinchy, County Down, Northern Ireland. Edward and his two younger brothers had brought with them a number of assisted emigrants from their father's estates. Ward's legal training was a great help to Godley, and they soon became good friends. Gouland, 'a wild-looking creature covered with hair' according to Ward, was already unpopular with the emigrants for trying to charge them customs duty on their personal possessions. Governor Grey had to intervene and overrule him.

Early in April 1851 Ward and Gouland dealt with the first great scandal of the new settlement, a refusal to work by the entire crew – John Nixon and 17 seamen – of the Canterbury Association's seventh ship, *Travancore*. Captain Henry Brown claimed to be mystified by the men's conduct, as he was generally satisfied with their work. He admitted he had had a quarrel with his first officer, Henry King, but none with the men. King told the JPs that in 10 years at sea he had never seen men treated so badly by a captain. They were 'driven hard', being kept at work night and day, even being taken out of their rest periods between watches. When questioned, one of the seamen said they had been 'treated like dogs'.

The first officer showed the magistrates the ship's log, with the entry of the men's refusal to work, and pointed out a previous assault by the captain on a man named Gardner. He had been slow to respond to an order to get in a studdingsail and 'made use of a bad oath' when the captain sharply repeated his order, whereupon

Captain Brown had boxed the man's ears, striking him open-handed on both sides of his head. The surgeon, John Livingstone, supported the captain, saying that he had observed 'no hard treatment' during the voyage to New Zealand, and the second mate, Edmund Smith, said that though the captain sometimes 'hurried them a little' they were not ill-used. Passengers Evans and Reeves agreed with these views. But the men still refused to return to work, and the captain discharged them.

When Ward ruled that each man should forfeit his wages and also his seafarer's clothes, Captain Brown then said that they might take their clothes, if they sent for them, as a gift. The *Travancore* remained at anchor until early June when, as Charlotte Godley tells us, it slipped away to Sydney in bad weather with only the surgeon and second mate from the original crew. Fresh hands had been signed on from the unemployed labourers and old lags of the port, keen to try their luck on the Australian goldfields.

Drunkenness was a major social problem in early Lyttelton, and Godley cracked down hard on anyone selling beer without a licence. Samuel Taylor had opened a restaurant where he was allowed to sell alcohol to accompany a meal, but early in April one of his customers was a policeman, Constable Samuel Madden, who testified that Taylor had charged him 2s for his dinner and a bottle of beer while several others bought beer but ordered no food. In short, Taylor was accused of running an illegal grog-shop. Christopher Dampier defended him ably, noting that 2s was a fair price for a dinner, and that it had been a house-warming party for the new restaurant. But Godley was unimpressed, and imposed a stiff £50 fine (some $5000 today), remarking that the case did not rely solely on the constable's testimony. In such a small community it was a safe bet that everybody knew what everybody else was up to. If Taylor could not find that sum, he would have been sent to the lockup. Or, like so many colonial miscreants, he may simply have disappeared to start again in another town.

Apart from seamen, most of the crimes in early Lyttelton were committed by ex-soldiers or former convicts. In May 1851 two former privates from the 65th Regiment, Adam Johnson and John Burgess, were accused of assault and robbery by their workmate, James Bannan. He said he had been walking home along the Sumner Road about 6.30 one evening when Johnson and Burgess joined him. Saying, 'Here's Bannan', Johnson put his hand in Bannan's pocket, but found nothing. They walked on for a dozen yards, then Johnson came up from behind and knocked Bannan to the ground 'with a blow and a kick'. Johnson put his knee on Bannan's stomach while Burgess removed 17s 6d from his other pocket. Johnson then said, 'Shall we throw him down the hill?', but Burgess said, 'No.' Both then made off, but Bannan had to spend the night with them in the whare they shared with other labourers: 'I did not dare leave them to give information, lest they should follow me. I had been drinking that night but was not drunk.'

In his defence, Johnson claimed Bannan was very drunk that night and had been involved in a fight in Lyttelton. He asserted that Bannan had started the altercation on the Sumner Road, but Bannan was able to provide three witnesses in support of his story, whereas Johnson and Burgess had none. Since these were serious offences, punishable until quite recently by transportation to Tasmania, Godley committed both prisoners for trial at the next Supreme Court. But there is no trace of their names in the *Lyttelton Times*, or the Wellington newspapers, suggesting that they may have absconded from the flimsy Lyttelton lockup and disappeared.

Godley lost his friend and fellow magistrate on 23 June 1851 when Edward Ward and his brother Henry were drowned in a boating accident near their Quail Island farm. This was lamented as a great loss to the young settlement, for Edward had impressed everyone as an able and energetic colonist, destined to become one of its leaders. His younger brother Hamilton stayed with the Godleys until another brother, Crosbie, came out to settle the brothers' affairs in June 1852. Crosbie Ward then bought a half-share in the *Lyttelton Times* and became the leading citizen that Edward never had a chance to become, as a member of parliament and cabinet minister, until his untimely death in 1867.

Godley was joined on the bench on 20 October 1851 by the association's emigration agent, James Edward FitzGerald, now sub-inspector
of police (and founding editor of the *Lyttelton Times*), to hear the most
complicated of Canterbury's early civil cases. Christopher Dampier
had leased 250 acres from the Reverend Benjamin Dudley on either
side of the Bridle Path above what was known for many years as
Dampiers Bay, and had been surprised to learn that a flock of 800
sheep and a herd of 66 cattle had been landed from the ship *Wellington*
and turned loose on his land without his permission. The owner of
the stock was a man named Kaye, who, according to his manager
Chapman and shepherds Cochrane, John Lockhart and McDonald,
had paid 5 guineas for the pasturage. Dampier informed them that
they were trespassing, as no arrangement had been made with him,
and after a few days the animals were taken over the Port Hills to
Christchurch.

In his defence Chapman said he was not aware that anyone
owned the land until he received a note from Dampier several days
after his arrival: 'Mr Dampier came to me on the Sunday, he asked
me to breakfast (laughter), he then said he should expect something'
for the sheep and cattle eating the pasture on his land. Kaye, who
was staying at the Mitre Hotel in Lyttelton, ordered Chapman to
remove the animals on the following Tuesday. Chapman added that
the sheep had strayed all over the hill, well beyond Dampier's leased
land.

Godley noted that this was an important case since it involved
the rights of everyone who rented pasturage in the settlement. The
Resident Magistrates' Ordinance of 1846 enabled him to decide on
'any claim for debt or damage' and gave him extended powers to hear
evidence and determine cases. He was satisfied that Dampier could
claim both damages for trespass and compensation for the two days
that had elapsed after his notice to Chapman. Godley thought the
trespass was probably inadvertent, and imposed a nominal fine of

5s, then calculated the reasonable amount for depasturage. As Kaye had not made an express bargain, nor shown any willingness to make an arrangement with Dampier, he should expect to pay the top rate of 2s 6d a week for the sheep and 1s a head for the cattle. For two days this came to £2 12s 5d (about $280). 'Every man must make his bargain himself; all that we say is that in the absence of a special bargain, which Mr. Kaye might have made if he had liked, it does not appear to us in the present case an unreasonable charge. As Mr. Kaye has made no tender of any payment, he must pay the costs.'

A couple of days earlier Dampier had appeared on behalf of the shepherd McDonald, who claimed that he was owed a premium by Kaye for having landed his stock safely. He had since been discharged and his wages paid, but McDonald 'gave a very different account of his agreement with Mr. Kaye from that which he had been paid upon'. The case lasted two hours, with arguments back and forth, but after being adjourned to 21 October it was then dismissed. Dampier himself had just been sued by the Canterbury Association's agent (Godley) for £12 unpaid balance on his purchase of a town section. Dampier objected that the conveyance did not include the payment of one-sixth to the Crown, or a proper receipt for this payment, but he was ordered to pay up. Dampier was determined to appeal against this decision.

Other cases in October included a breach of promise of marriage (5s damages with costs), cutting timber without a licence (ditto), building a house within a disputed boundary (ditto), and unpaid rent for a stable and the keep of a horse, which resulted in surveyor Charles Torlesse paying Alfred Lake £1 3s 6d.

This was not a good month for Torlesse. He was back before the magistrates on 18 October to answer a claim of £10 for the loss of a valuable dog, brought by a Maori named Tinui (probably Tainui) from the native reserve at Rapaki. Torlesse admitted shooting the dog, but said that dogs from the reserve had done much injury to his sheep, and that a Maori named Solomon had given him permission to kill them. Solomon, however, said that he had qualified this per-mission as applying only to *bad* dogs, whereas Mr Torlesse had shot a very good dog, which was certainly worth £10. The dog had been killed near the Maori pa, and not on Torlesse's run. The magistrates awarded the claimant £2 in damages. This case is a good example of Maori readiness to use the courts to seek redress for loss or injury.

Late in 1851 Godley's private secretary, James Wortley, resigned to go off sheep farming and was replaced by a young family friend, Charles Christopher Bowen, who had been a law student at Cambridge when he suddenly decided to join his aunt and parents and emigrate to Canterbury on the *Charlotte Jane*. Impressed by this polite and capable young man, Godley appointed him a justice of the peace in 1852. (Bowen would become a magistrate in 1864 and minister of justice in 1874, ending his days as Sir Christopher Bowen and one of the architects of New Zealand's education system.)

Godley was absent for a tobacco smuggling case in February 1852, heard by Captain Charles Simeon and FitzGerald. A man named McDonald was charged with a breach of the customs laws, by having 29lbs (13kg) of illicit tobacco in his possession. McDonald was defended by Dampier, who raised a preliminary objection on the ground that the information had been laid before the resident magistrate alone, instead of two justices. This technical objection was overruled.

The key witness was James Tregear, who said he was woken about 2 or 3 o'clock on the morning of 10 February by a dog barking. He saw a man come past a V-hut and close by Mr Birch's house. It was a fine moonlit night, and he recognised the man as McDonald, who then returned and came past the back of Cookson's premises, emerging from under a ladder with something under his arm. Tregear followed him into the gully, and saw him drop something. A few yards further on he tackled McDonald and there was a scuffle. He called for help and within a few minutes the watchman and Constable Hugh Bracken came up. When Tregear said he thought the parcel had been taken from Cookson's store, Bracken arrested McDonald and searched the ground. A parcel of tobacco, 'negrohead or cavendish', was found, and later handed over to sub-collector of customs William Eades. He weighed it and put it in the bond store.

Joseph Clarkson attempted to give an alternative explanation that would let McDonald off the charge, saying he had found a bundle near the watercourse that Tuesday, which McDonald identified as his. It contained two shirts. Recalled to the witness stand, Tregear said that McDonald had nothing with him when he passed the V-hut, and that the parcel he then saw him carrying was much larger than two shirts would be. The magistrates considered the offence proved, and asked Eades to decide between the statutory penalty of £100 ($10,000 today) or treble the value of the tobacco. Tobacco of that quality was worth 5s or 6s a pound, so Eades opted for the lesser sum (about £21). The magistrates agreed, and allowed time for payment.

A spectacular neighbourhood scrap in Lyttelton ended in court in May 1852 before JPs FitzGerald and Isaac Cookson. Jane Frost testified that she had stepped out of her house the previous Thursday to drive her chickens in. When Henry Presley asked who she was calling devils, and she replied that she was speaking to her children (possibly a misprint for chickens?) he said, 'Get off the path, you dirty bundle!' She refused. Jane Frost told the court: 'He assaulted and kicked me, Mrs. Presley flew at me, and tore my bonnet off. I said nothing to provoke Presley beyond saying I would not go off the path; I was not on his garden ground; Mrs. P. broke my bonnet before I tore her cap.'

Another neighbour, Charlotte Loder, confirmed Mrs Frost's testimony, but admitted she did not see her first tear Susannah Presley's cap off, nor scratch Mr Presley's face. Hester Clarkson also saw the parties fighting: Mr Presley was throwing half-bricks at Mrs Frost's fowls, and in return Mrs Frost hurled a lump of dirt at Presley. Ann Witton said she heard Presley abusing Mrs Frost, and saw the parties fighting. Mrs Presley had struck Mrs Frost first. W. Bennett, however, claimed that Mrs Frost struck first and grabbed Mrs Presley's cap. D. Diamond saw the women fighting, and heard Presley encourage his wife to 'go on': 'they were pulling each other's hair when I first saw them'.

In his own defence Henry Presley said he had asked Mrs Frost to keep her fowls off his garden, but she had called him a devil and said she would not: 'I threatened to kill them; she called me "an ugly-looking devil" and threatened to kill me.' Susannah Presley supported her husband's testimony: 'Mrs Frost struck and scratched him; afterwards scratched me.' The magistrates were more inclined to accept Mrs Frost's testimony, and fined Henry Presley £1 and Susannah Presley 10s, with costs. After such open hostilities and heavy fines, one wonders which of the neighbours moved house first.

A few days later, on 15 May, a full bench of magistrates sat in Christchurch to hear a case of assault that had taken place at John and William Deans' farm in Riccarton. This appears to be the first such court held in Christchurch. Godley was joined by his fellow magistrate, Captain Simeon, and JPs Mark Stoddart and Edward Jerningham Wakefield (only son of E. G. Wakefield). They must have sat very close together, for the courtroom was a cramped upstairs room in the Land Office on Oxford Terrace. George Dalton, a farm worker, whose face 'exhibited marks of desperate punishment', accused Samuel Duffty of assaulting him on the previous Tuesday evening:

> I, with three or four others, was in the kitchen, we were all good company having a game of cards over a glass of grog. Duffty came in about 11 o'clock; he was drunk, and became quarrelsome. My wife told the girl to go to bed, as it was not fit for her to sit there in the company of drunken men. Duffty turned to my wife and swore he would wring her nose off and mine too, and would take it out of me ... he struck me a severe blow which felled me, and he then set to kicking me, until I called out for assistance.

When Captain Simeon asked Dalton if he had said anything to aggravate Duffty, he replied, 'None whatever, the only thing at which he could be at all offended was my wife ordering the girl go off to bed.' At Godley's request, Dalton then swore that there was no provocation on his part. At this point Duffty interrupted and asked, 'Did you not call me a convict and a transport?' Dalton denied this.

Other witnesses supported Dalton's testimony. Surveyor Thomas

Cass said he heard a shout of 'Murder!' and came out to see the men fighting: 'There was a great deal of talking between them ... Duffty was extremely abusive and used frightful language.' Cass added that Duffty had previously caused a disturbance at the Deans farm and had been dismissed, but was later rehired. Charles Roe heard Duffty say, 'I'll teach you to be quiet.' He saw Duffty striking Dalton, and helped Cass to stop him. Godley said that, having heard all of the evidence, the affair appeared to be an unprovoked assault, and he fined Duffty 50s with costs.

Godley then left the bench and returned as a prosecutor against Thomas Hardy and Phillip Woodford, neither of whom appeared. They had apparently been squatting on public reserves and building huts, one in Hagley Park and the other on the bank of the Avon River between the Bricks and the Market Place. They had been ordered several times to remove themselves, but had so often broken their promises that Godley had instructed Constable Connell to serve them with a summons for trespass. Godley tabled a copy of the summons, and his brother magistrates agreed to fine each man 10s with costs.

Horses were extremely valuable animals in these early years, but one Maori litigant in June 1852 failed to get any compensation for the loss of his steed. His name was Daniel and he spoke in Maori, with John Marshman interpreting. He had taken his horse to the Christchurch Livery Stables to be treated for an injury, and the owner, Thomas Jackson, had said it would take two weeks. They agreed on an amount to be paid, and when Daniel came back after a week to see the horse, he saw it was recovering well. When he arrived to collect it a week later, however, Jackson said it had broken from its tether and could not be found. A search was started and the horse was found dead, having drowned in a swamp. Daniel claimed the enormous sum of £28 in compensation, which Jackson refused to pay.

The magistrates took a long time over this case, because its outcome could affect every horse-owner in the settlement. The verbal agreement 'was gone into very minutely'. They established that Daniel was aware the horse was to be tethered out, as he could not afford the cost of stabling and stable feed, and that Jackson was paid merely for treating the horse's bad back. Jackson insisted that he was not responsible for the horse's loss and the magistrates agreed, dismissing the case. Though it was hard on Daniel, who had lost his horse, the magistrates thought he had probably deliberately inflated its real value.

Godley last appeared as a magistrate in Christchurch on 21 June 1852, when he sat with Captain Richard Westenra, Jerningham Wakefield, and Messrs William Bray, William Guise Brittan and John Watts Russell, to hear a case of wilful damage to a valuable cow. Bartholomew Flanagan was charged with shooting a cow belonging to Henry Francis Worsley, who testified that the animal was scarcely able to move and was likely to die. A neighbour said Flanagan had asked him about a fortnight before for two charges of powder and shot, to frighten cows away from his garden. S. Stephens testified that when he had met Flanagan ditching outside his garden, the latter had said, 'If I see any cows in my garden I'll pepper them, as I have got a gun loaded.' Stephens had passed this information on to his neighbour, Walpole Fendall, who had a joint interest in the cow with Worsley. Fendall went to warn Flanagan that he had no right to shoot any cows since his garden was not properly fenced. Flanagan replied that he had shot at a black bull, but not at the red cow. Fendall went immediately to the spot, about 100 yards from Flanagan's garden, and found the injured cow. The black bull showed no signs of having been shot. Another witness said he had seen Flanagan try at the cow twice, but the gun had misfired.

Asked by Godley if he had anything to say, Flanagan 'denied most positively having shot at the cow'. The court was cleared and the magistrates deliberated for some time. When the press reporters were allowed back, Godley told Flanagan there was insufficient evidence to send the case before a jury, and he would therefore be discharged. But, Godley added,

I wish you to know that there are grave suspicions on our minds. The offence is one which, when the offender is convicted, brings with it the sentence of transportation to Van Diemen's Land [Tasmania], and we give this warning, as a belief appears to exist that owners of land are justified in shooting at cattle trespassing. Every trespass subjects owners of cattle to legal damages, but it lies at the discretion of the magistrates to award nominal damages, or otherwise, according to the sufficiency of the fence around the land trespassed upon.

Godley's work as a magistrate is barely mentioned by his biographer, C. E. Carrington, and is only briefly acknowledged by Gerald Hensley in his entry in *The Dictionary of New Zealand Biography*.[2] They are, quite properly, much more concerned with his role in the establishment of the settlement and his administration of land policy. Godley's greatest decision was to bend the Canterbury Association's restrictive rules for pastoral leases. Wakefield's roseate vision of a compact agricultural settlement simply did not work in the harsh realities of colonial life. Godley saw that the province's best export would be wool, and therefore bypassed the law to allow large areas of the country to be taken up for grazing sheep. He often clashed with Grey over land policy, but he held firm, and wool soon became the basis of the Canterbury economy.

Godley had never intended to settle in New Zealand. Indeed, he tried to resign in 1851 but was persuaded to stay until the New Zealand Constitution Act was proclaimed and Canterbury had its own government as one of the original six provinces. Some of his friends wanted him to be the first superintendent but he declined, and the Godleys departed in December 1852. His friend FitzGerald was then elected superintendent in 1853. Godley always said that the association's job was to establish the settlement, not to govern it. He had certainly done that, and had also been a de facto governor.

Getting the machinery of the courts and police in place to ensure law and order was the major achievement he shared with FitzGerald.

After his return to England, Godley was appointed to the War Office as director-general of stores, to help sort out the mess that had developed in the early phase of the Crimean War, and in 1857 he was appointed assistant under-secretary of state for war. As his friends had noticed, he was a glutton for work and a brilliant administrator, but a chronic throat infection undermined his health and he died in November 1861. When the news reached Christchurch, his many friends raised a public subscription for a statue, and Lord Lyttelton commissioned the leading British sculptor of the day, Thomas Woolner. When the work, New Zealand's oldest public statue, was unveiled by C. C. Bowen in Cathedral Square in 1867, it was declared an excellent likeness. In 1918 it was moved to a new site on the eastern side of the cathedral, to make way for a bus shelter, but it was returned to its original location in 1933. The Godley statue fell over in the February 2011 Christchurch earthquake, and for a short while the bronze Godley had his nose on the ground, until he was taken away for restoration.[3]

CHAPTER TWO

RUN, RONAGE, RUN!

Edward William Seager
(1828–1922), deputy
immigration officer
and police sergeant
at Lyttelton, then first
keeper and steward of the
Sunnyside Lunatic Asylum,
Christchurch, where he
introduced humane and
advanced methods for
treating the mentally
ill. He was later usher
at the Supreme Court,
Christchurch.

Cyclopedia of New Zealand,
vol. 3, Canterbury, 1903

A t the time of Godley's farewell, Christchurch was little more than a straggling wooden village scattered across a flat, open, treeless site. Captain Thomas and his surveyors had pegged out the streets of the future city in a north-south grid pattern across the meandering Avon River, reserving a large public domain and park (now Hagley Park and the Botanic Gardens) between the Canterbury Association settlement and the Deans' farm. The migrants had paid for an option on both rural land and a town section, and there was much interest in the selection of plots at the Land Office on 17 February 1851. A small footbridge beside the office was at first the only way to cross the river dry-shod. Some months later a cart bridge was built in the Market Place, but until then most people crossed on horseback, for the water was deep, and very cold.

Hammering and sawing must have been among the commonest noises in Christchurch during 1851, as the migrants built themselves cottages, houses and shops. Some of the timber came from the Papanui Bush, which was entirely cut out within a few years, but most was imported from the North Island or Tasmania. Wooden shingles formed the rooftops until corrugated iron became the norm for colonial buildings. Horses were scarce, and valuable, in the early days of settlement, and the roads were little more than tracks, dusty in summer and muddy in winter. Most people simply walked, often for hours on end, to get from Lyttelton to their Christchurch sections. With no cart road over the Port Hills, heavy goods had to be brought round by sea to Sumner, to risk the river bar at the entrance to the broad estuary of the Avon and Heathcote rivers. This was a dangerous crossing, and even large sailing boats were easily wrecked.

As we have seen, Godley and his fellow magistrates occasionally held court in the Land Office when there were cases to be heard in Christchurch, but anybody sentenced to imprisonment had to be escorted over the hill to the flimsy wooden gaol at Lyttelton. This establishment finally acquired a dedicated and capable keeper at the end of 1851 in the person of Edward William Seager, a friend of FitzGerald, who appointed him deputy immigration officer, police constable and gaolkeeper. Seager was to become a legend in his own lifetime, rising to head the small police force at Lyttelton, becoming sub-inspector of police in 1858 and then the first warden of Sunnyside Asylum on the outskirts of Christchurch from 1863 to 1887.

Seager was a big man, scrupulously honest and hard-working, with a deep commitment to public service and reform. Prisoners found him a fair and humane gaoler, concerned for their welfare and improvement. He was a talented musician with a passion for the theatre, and at Sunnyside he was well ahead of his time in organising occupational therapy, plays and concerts for the mentally ill. He also had a great sense of humour; one family story concerns the flimsy wooden Lyttelton lockup.

Some sailors who had refused to work were held in the gaol until they appeared before the magistrate. One evening the armed constable standing guard reported to Seager that he had seen the lockup move. Seager and the other constables came up from the police barracks in time to see the lockup rise from its site and start moving down the hill. The sailors had kicked holes in the floor for their feet and were lifting the small building off the ground. But in the darkness they could not see where they were going. Seager, who enjoyed practical jokes, whispered to the constables to fetch some stakes, which they drove into the ground on either side of the slowly moving structure, gently guiding its progress towards the police barracks. Once alongside, they threw ropes over the hut and the moving gaol was 'safely brought to anchorage'. The magistrate ordered the men back to work on the ship, but some of them later deserted and disappeared.

This amusing but embarrassing episode made it imperative for the association to start building a proper gaol for Lyttelton. It was designed by William Chaney, a stonemason who had come out on the *Randolph* to work on the proposed cathedral, but the diocese had no money for this major project for many years to come. He designed a stocky two-storey building with battlements and a cross at one end, which made it look like a chapel. A high masonry wall went up around the exercise yard to make escapes more difficult. The hard-labour gang helped to build it but progress was slow, and in the meantime a three-cell lockup with solid clay walls was hastily erected by Charles Crawford. Even brawny sailors would have trouble getting this to move down the hill. This lockup did duty for another decade, as the new gaol was not finally completed until 1861.

But clay walls were not enough to keep some prisoners confined. Seager was on guard duty one stormy night in the winter of 1852, armed with a carbine and bayonet, when he noticed a dark patch on the wall of the gaol. On closer inspection he discovered it was a large hole. The prisoner, who had been confined as a 'lunatic', had patiently scraped a hole in the wall with his tin pannikin and departed. He was never seen again, and it was presumed that he had drowned while crossing a river. 'Missing, Presumed Drowned' was by far the commonest cause of death in colonial New Zealand.

The first sitting of a Supreme Court in Christchurch was held early in November 1852 in the schoolroom of the temporary Church of St Michael and All Angels, which served as the town's pro-cathedral until 1881. Sidney Stephen, who was resident judge for the newly created Southern District of New Zealand, had come down from Wellington, and sat flanked by Captain Simeon as resident magistrate and Edward Wright, the sheriff, who was properly dressed in black stockings and white ruffles. The court was formally opened by the crier with the traditional formula of 'Hear ye, hear ye ...', before the registrar called the names of the grand jury and 15 worthy gentlemen responded. The judge directed them to elect a foreman, and Isaac Thomas Cookson JP was duly elected. The judge complimented the jurors on their punctual attendance, considering the shortness of the notice they had received, then delivered 'a rather lengthy charge', in which he 'entered very minutely' on the cases to be heard.

The first case was a charge of breaking and entering, with theft of blankets from David Laurie's store on Norwich Quay in Lyttelton. George Johnston had sold some blankets to Richard Taylor of the Robin Hood Hotel, which Laurie later identified as the ones stolen from his store. Johnston conducted his own defence, and appears to have done so very ably. Laurie had to admit that there were hundreds of similar blankets in the town and that his had no particular identifying marks. He further admitted that Taylor had spoken to him a few days after the robbery and said he thought he knew who had done it – either George or William Johnston. He had then told FitzGerald, as sub-inspector of police, and the blankets had been recovered from the Robin Hood. In his defence Johnston said he was innocent, but had had an argument with Taylor since selling him the blankets, and had threatened to thrash him. He alleged that Taylor had laid this charge against him in spiteful retaliation.

The jury returned a verdict of not guilty, after a very brief retirement, and the judge agreed that the case had been poorly presented. But Johnston was not a free man. He faced another charge, of stealing a watch, and came before the court again on 9 November. (In the meantime he had attempted to escape from gaol.) This time the evidence was conclusive, from several reputable witnesses, and the jury had no hesitation in returning a guilty verdict. The judge sentenced him to seven years' transportation to Tasmania.

The same sentence was passed on another prisoner, George Godwin, who was charged with larceny as a servant. He was shopman for a draper, John Fraser, who noticed that various items had gone missing from the shop over a long period; Godwin was the prime suspect. The police searched the house where he lodged and found a large number of collars, velvets, ribbons and waistcoat pieces. Georgiana Wilkin said that Godwin had always claimed he bought these items at sales, and made no attempt to conceal them, but Edward Genet testified that he had received from the prisoner, for sale or return, a spirit flask and loose cutlery that Fraser identified as his. In summing up, the judge remarked that Fraser conducted his business in an 'extremely loose way', which gave the prisoner ample opportunity for dishonesty, and remarked that it had been difficult to get accurate or intelligent evidence from Fraser: 'not of a desire to be obscure, but rather of a want of facility of comprehension – a crassness of mind, as it were'. (We may wonder if Fraser fully comprehended the judge's condescending insult.) With no secure gaol in Lyttelton, Mr Justice Stephen took the two condemned prisoners back to Wellington with him.

The last case of the Criminal Sessions in 1852 was an accusation of libel brought by Christopher Dampier against FitzGerald and William Guise Brittan, claiming £500 in damages for publishing the minutes of a meeting of the Council of Land Purchasers in May 1851, in which it was suggested that Dampier had tried to induce the contractor to alter the line of the road from the Heathcote Ferry so as to enlarge the size of his section between the Ferry Road and the river.

The scandal of a libel case had produced 'considerable excitement' in the small Christchurch community, and the court was 'thronged', especially by 'several of the fairer portion of creation'. It was a splendid entertainment to see public figures squabbling in public. In essence, Dampier claimed that the survey of the road reserve was inaccurate, and differed from the boundary he had seen on the map that accompanied Land Order 32. When the road was pegged out, his section had been narrowed significantly, including the most valuable part, suitable for future wharves and warehouses. He had remonstrated with the contractor and complained to the surveyor, Edward Jollie. Chief Surveyor Thomas Cass admitted that a mistake had been made, probably as a result of somebody moving the poles, but added that orders had been given (by whom it was not said) to make the road straight and touch the river at the two bends. Brittan had then suggested that Dampier might abandon his riverside section and choose another somewhere else. Dampier refused, and demanded an independent survey, but Brittan would not agree.

When Dampier moved to have the offensive words removed from the minutes, FitzGerald proposed a counter-motion, which was carried at the council meeting of 31 May, approving the minutes of 26 May. However, the judge pointed out that since the charge was against both Brittan and FitzGerald, the plaintiff had to prove joint composing and joint publication, as the damages were indivisible. Questioning of the clerk to the Council of Land Purchasers failed to prove that the defendants were joint parties to the publication of the libel, and Dampier's counsel elected to be non-suited.[1] Dampier's case had collapsed.

This complicated courtroom drama must have caused a great deal of debate and bad feeling, for both sides had their supporters, equally convinced they were in the right. Though a gentleman by birth, Dampier was not socially acceptable to the Godley–FitzGerald camp because he was notoriously litigious and increasingly spoke up for artisans and workmen. This libel action left a 'black mark' against him among the most respectable section of the settler elite. According to Henry Sewell, his knowledge of the law was surprisingly incomplete, but he was easily the most active lawyer in early Canterbury, taking on cases that nobody else would touch.

Dampier's greatest triumph in 1853 was his defence of James Murrey, landlord of the Travellers' Home, which later became the famous Nancy's Hotel by Hagley Park. He had been charged, on the information of 'the notorious Bill Holland', with serving drinks after hours at night and selling spirits on a Sunday morning. This case aroused 'the greatest excitement' in Christchurch, and the Magistrate's Court was 'very much crowded'. Dampier's cross-examination of Holland's witnesses revealed more than Holland might have wished. It appeared that he was trying to take over the livery stables behind the White Hart Hotel, but was short of the asking price and before he could close the deal he needed to 'raise the wind' by some means or other.

The key witness was George Long, who told the court that Holland had promised to make his fortune and show him 'where to find gold' if he testified that Murrey had served him after 10pm. The court was cleared and the magistrates conferred. When the court reconvened, Captain Simeon dismissed the charge, adding that 'the nature of the evidence brought before us leaves little doubt but that the whole affair has been a base attempt at conspiracy and bribery'. Thomas Jackson of the Christchurch Livery Stables asked permission to make a statement, as he had 'found out the secret that had been plotted against Mr Murrey, and wished to expose the villainous conspiracy that had been got up by certain parties to injure [him] and extort money from an honest man's pocket'.

Captain Simeon said that would not be necessary, as the bench was 'perfectly satisfied', and Mr Murrey left the court without the slightest stain on his character. 'The notorious Bill Holland' seems to have taken himself off smartly, before any charges could be laid against him, as there is no further mention of him in the *Lyttelton Times*.

In November 1853 Seager was promoted to sergeant and two additional constables were assigned to help him keep order in Christchurch. On his visits from Lyttelton to supervise them he lodged in a tiny lean-to behind John Dilloway's premises at the corner of Armagh and Colombo streets. With no lockup in Christchurch, he had to march any prisoners over the hill to the Lyttelton Gaol. On one stormy night, having arrested a runaway convict in Riccarton, he got his man to the ferry at Ferrymead, where he fired his gun to attract the ferrykeeper's attention. The exhausted prisoner fell to his knees and pleaded, 'Master, master, for God's sake don't shoot me!' On another occasion, having arrested a disorderly drunkard, Seager handcuffed the man to the verandah post of the Golden Fleece Hotel while he went in search of a constable to help him.

Seager became famous in the little community for his ingenuity and many arrests. In 1854 he boarded a ship in Lyttelton to investigate the loss of a chamois bag containing 70 gold sovereigns, the property of a passenger named Julian. The head steward, Samuel Smith, was the leading suspect, as he had been spending sovereigns in Lyttelton even though the crew had not yet been paid off. Seager obtained a warrant to search Smith's cabin, but found nothing incriminating in his trunk. Then he had an idea. When he measured the depth of the trunk, first on the outside and then on the inside, there was a difference of several inches. Seager then opened the false bottom and there was the chamois bag. Smith was sentenced to five years with hard labour.

For Seager and his constables, and the goggle-eyed population of Lyttelton, 1855 was dominated by the arrest, trial and several escapes of a Gaelic-speaking Scots shepherd James Mackenzie (also spelt McKenzie), who was charged with stealing 1000 sheep from George Rhodes's sheep station, The Levels, inland from Timaru. This was a famous case, and has been much written about, including a novel by James McNeish.

Robert Heaton Rhodes and George Rhodes were the younger brothers of William Barnard Rhodes, a whaler who had visited what was then Port Cooper in the 1830s. William had climbed to the top of the Port Hills and viewed the future site of Christchurch, declaring it a vast swamp covered in water, with two patches of bush – Riccarton and Papanui. He saw better prospects at Akaroa Harbour, where he purchased land from local Maori and later landed the first herd of cattle in the South Island at Red House Bay. William, also known as Captain Rhodes, or plain 'Barney' Rhodes, then established himself in Wellington, where he became one of its wealthiest merchants and land speculators – they called him 'the millionaire of Wellington'. The three brothers had bought the Purau run from the Greenwoods and, as we have seen, Robert and George were farming there when the First Four Ships of the Canterbury Association arrived in December 1850. Anxious in case the association failed to recognise their land claims, Robert and George took a large mob of sheep to South Canterbury, to set up a station outside the Canterbury Block (the land purchased from Maori by the Canterbury Association), inland from the future site of Timaru.

The basin now known as the Mackenzie Country was then undiscovered, and it was later assumed that Mackenzie hid his stolen sheep there. Most people assumed he was guilty because he tried to escape, but it now seems possible that he was 'framed' by the drunken and incompetent young 'gentleman' John Sidebottom, overseer at The Levels, to conceal his shady dealings with nearby runholders. He and two Maori shepherds captured Mackenzie, who then escaped and walked all the way to Lyttelton, where Seager found him in an attic. He had a gun, but Seager already had him 'covered'. Seager claimed never to have forgotten the shepherd's piercing blue eyes.

Mackenzie spoke fluent Gaelic, but in court claimed that he did not understand English. He refused to cooperate with an interpreter who had links with the Rhodes family. The only time he showed any emotion was when confronted by his faithful dog Friday, who later became George Rhodes's favourite dog at The Levels. Mackenzie had no defence counsel, and the judge seemed to assume that the prisoner was guilty until proven innocent. Mackenzie's silence was declared 'mute of malice', the jury declared him guilty and he was sentenced to five years in prison. He made three escape attempts, but each time was found and brought back to Lyttelton, insisting on his innocence. This pattern was becoming so embarrassing to the government that he was given a pardon in 1856 on condition that he leave the colony. He did so, and was never heard of again.

The next three years were dominated by the antics of another persistent escaper, an exceptionally troublesome and violent prisoner named Alfred Ronage. (That was how he wrote his name, but the newspapers spelt it Ronnage.) In July 1856 Ronage was arrested and charged with the assault and highway robbery of James Nelson near the Royal Hotel one Saturday night. Nelson had his jaw broken and his silver watch taken, along with some money and articles of clothing. The watch was easily identified: it had a silver chain and a seal showing a storm-tossed ship with the motto 'Such is Life'. The police assumed that Ronage was also behind a robbery at Gartner's house on Papanui Road. The *Lyttelton Times* reported that he had already made himself notorious in Akaroa by his frequent breaches of the law. He was now taken to the Lyttelton Gaol, where his behaviour was described as 'silly' and 'outrageous'. He made so much trouble for Seager that he was put in leg-irons.

In September 1856, however, Ronage used a knife to saw through the chain – the newspaper remarked that this was the second time he had managed to do this – and escaped from the exercise yard when the warder's back was turned. He ran off up the gully behind the gaol, but was soon caught, and a heavier set of leg-irons was padlocked to his ankles. In court on 11 March 1857 he was given two years for a previous robbery and one year for attempting to escape, but the more serious charge of highway robbery was reserved for the next sitting of the Supreme Court later that month.

Ronage defended himself, with boldness and good humour.

The prosecutor was Henry Barnes Gresson, an Irish lawyer who had come to Christchurch in 1854. (He was unlucky enough to lose his personal baggage and family silver when the *Palmer* was wrecked on the Sumner Bar.) Everyone thought well of Gresson, Charles Torlesse describing him as 'a prodigy here – an honest lawyer'. Gresson noted that the police case lacked evidence, and relied mostly on assumption and hearsay. The jury, not believing that any felonious intent had been proven, let Ronage off the robbery charge and recommended a light sentence for the assault. The judge disagreed, and sentenced him to 12 months' hard labour: 'He hoped the light sentence would have a permanent good effect.' As the *Lyttelton Times* remarked drily, 'Our old acquaintance Ronnage has been found less guilty than was expected, a sentimental jury having ignored the greatest part of his crime, much to the astonishment of court and prisoner.'

Ronage had written to the provincial government, asking to be relieved of his irons, in view of the prompt capture of another runaway convict named Sullivan in 1857. Seager and his men were so vigilant, Ronage implied, that nobody had a chance to get clear away. His letter shows him to be a man of some education and intelligence. Readers of the newspapers found all this most amusing, but Seager was taking no chances and Ronage, whom he described as 'dangerous, and never safe at any time', went back into irons.[2]

To everyone's astonishment, Ronage made another break for freedom in October 1857, with the help of a prisoner named Charles Thomas Smith. They were with a work gang on the Sumner Road when the constable on duty turned his back to attend to a call of nature. Ronage and Smith broke into the overseer's hut and stole two loaded carbines, before making off up the track towards Evans Pass. Presumably they also relieved Ronage of his leg-irons. They held up at gunpoint the terrified housekeeper at the Reverend George Cotterill's house, and took some food, then went over the hill towards Sumner.

Seager armed himself and two constables, and set off in pursuit. They rested near a large rock, where Seager heard rustling in the flax below them. He whispered to the constables that he would go out into the open and if the convicts fired he would pretend to be hit by throwing his arms up. The plan worked. Seager shouted 'I'm shot!' and fell to the ground. Ronage and Smith came out of hiding and the constables called on them to surrender. When they refused, Seager fired on Smith from his prone position, hitting him in the thigh. Ronage ran off down the valley with the constables' bullets whistling past him. Seager bound up Smith's wound and borrowed a horse to take him back to Lyttelton. Meanwhile the constables followed Ronage for two hours, down the valley and as far as Shag Rock, where he jumped into the sea. The tide then carried him back towards Cave Rock, where the constables dragged him from the water, too exhausted to resist arrest. They bound his wrists with flax and walked him back over the hill to Lyttelton.

John Hall, Canterbury's commissioner of police, recommended a reward of £5 to Seager and £3 to Corporal Charles Rutledge – the Armed Constabulary used military ranks – for their bravery and determination in recapturing these two escapees. But the convicts probably thought they deserved some recognition for their determination as well. Smith, on crutches while his leg wound healed, was allowed to exercise with no special guard, as he was considered unlikely to escape, but escape he did one afternoon, up the hill towards the cemetery. Seager ran after him, but lost him near Captain Simeon's house. The most likely bolthole was Simeon's stable. Seager looked inside, noticed a small trapdoor leading to the hayloft, called out, as if to a non-existent constable, 'Well, he's not here, I'll have to give up', then hid and waited. After a long pause, Smith's legs appeared in the opening. Seager grabbed him and advised him to come quietly, but Smith fought savagely, biting Seager's face and wrist, shouting, 'It's either you or me for it!' Seager managed to head-butt and partially stun Smith, then bound his hands with a rope from the stable wall. Smith was still kicking when Captain Simeon's groom came to see what all the noise was about. He helped Seager to bathe his bleeding head and wrapped a towel around it. When Smith faced the magistrate a few days later, Seager made light of the affray, knowing that Smith could be given up to two years in irons for assaulting a prison warder. He was given six months' hard labour, with one month in solitary confinement.

By the time Ronage came up for trial in March 1858, Gresson had been appointed a judge of the Supreme Court, with jurisdiction over the entire South Island. Ronage again conducted his own defence, claiming extenuating circumstances, namely that he was mentally deranged at the time. He also alleged that the police were to blame for not doing their duty and keeping a sufficiently strict guard over him. This time the jury was not amused, and found him guilty of escape and robbery. Nor was Gresson much amused: he sentenced Ronage to three years with hard labour.

Yet still the incorrigible Ronage tried to escape. In September 1858 he made a break from a labour gang, but this time his previous partner Smith immediately told Constable J. Arnold, and Ronage was recaptured straight away. Smith had decided to behave himself, and became such an exemplary prisoner that in August 1859, when he petitioned for early release, he was supported by Dr Donald as the gaol's medical officer and visiting JP. One of the warders, James Reston, who was to follow Seager as head gaoler, also wrote in support of Smith's petition, which was granted. He was released in November 1859 and the locals raised a public subscription to pay his passage to Sydney, to make sure they were rid of him.

Encouraged by Smith's success, Ronage also wrote to the provincial superintendent, William Moorhouse, pleading for release from his 'long and painful imprisonment'. He had by now been wearing heavy leg-irons for over two years. Though he promised good behaviour his petition failed, and he presumably served out his time. Ronage disappears from the record, so he may have gone to Sydney as well.

But he was not forgotten in Canterbury, where he had provided sensational news and entertainment for three years in a row. He was immortalised in verse by Crosbie Ward, in the opening stanza of his famous satire 'The Sumner Road':

The Sumner Road! The Sumner Road!
Which burly Thomas first began;
Where Dobson all his skill bestowed,
FitzGerald drove and Ronnage ran.
Eternal talking still goes on;
But nothing save the talk is done.[3]

CHAPTER THREE

THE RICCARTON POISONING OF 1859

THE POLICE.
'I tell yer what, Bill; I think the police are a bad lot, and I wish they was done away with altogether.'

John Leech,
Four Hundred Humorous Illustrations,
2nd edn, 1862

James Gregg was a quarryman in Scotland when he married Christina Ferguson in 1834, in the parish of East Kilbride, Lanarkshire. She was aged 20 and he was her senior by more than two decades. They had no children, and nothing is known of their life until they arrived in Nelson in 1842. The Greggs farmed at Stoke, but, like all the Nelson settlers, they had a hard struggle. They were all too poor to buy each other's produce and the economy was slow to get started, so it is not surprising that when he heard of the Canterbury settlement Gregg decided to travel south and seek work among Captain Thomas's carpenters and labourers. At Lyttelton he formed a partnership with Thomas Jackson Hughes, the foreman of a drain-digging gang, and they undertook the work of levelling the slope alongside Oxford Street for the immigration barracks. The Greggs were given permission to squat on a section in Exeter Street. Gregg was described by one of his contemporaries as 'a singular specimen of a colonist: shrewd, industrious, comical, and extremely independent'.[1]

Gregg tendered for the construction of the seawall with Robert Allan, but then withdrew and joined a roadworks gang. By January 1851 Hughes had gained the contract to operate the punt at Ferrymead, and Gregg, as an experienced quarryman, may have been involved in metalling the newly formed Ferry Road. During 1851 he was involved in contract work on several major roads in Riccarton, Papanui and the Styx, and is said to have helped build the first cart bridge over the Avon at the Market Place.

Christina became pregnant in 1851 and gave birth to a son, christened James after his father. She was now 36, and they seemed a happy little family. By 1853 Gregg had done well enough to buy a 50-acre (20ha) section and to start building a house, Woodside Farm, on what is now the corner of Riccarton Road and Matipo Street. By 1858 he was employing a young farm labourer named Edmund Langstreth, who boarded in the house with the Greggs.

James Gregg died at his Riccarton house on 11 October 1859 at the age of 65 after a short but violent illness. After rumours began to circulate about the death Dr Donald, as coroner for the Canterbury district, held an inquest at the Plough Inn (as the Travellers' Home was now known) two days later, behind closed doors. The coroner's court heard that Gregg had been into town on Monday 10 October and had returned that evening, apparently in good health. He had had a game of marbles with his young son, then went to bed as cheerful as usual about 10pm. During the night, however, he became violently ill, vomiting and purging. He complained of a burning heat in his stomach, and asked for water, which Mrs Gregg gave him constantly throughout the night, but he refused to send for the doctor. When he got worse towards morning, and collapsed after trying to walk to the toilet, Christina Gregg called Langstreth to help her, and managed to get him back into bed.

Langstreth was then dispatched to fetch Dr Thomas Fisher, who arrived about 9am. By that time Gregg was in a very bad way, still conscious but unable to speak. Fisher considered the case hopeless, but wrote a prescription and sent Langstreth into town for the medicine and some brandy. On his return Mrs Gregg offered her husband some of the brandy in hot water, but he died without tasting it. Christina Gregg then sent for her brother, John Ferguson, who came at once and offered to make the coffin. Because the death had been unusual and sudden, Dr Fisher came back, removed the stomach from the body and took it away for a post-mortem examination.

Dr Donald adjourned the inquest until the Saturday, so that the results of the post-mortem could be considered. Dr Fisher and Dr Turnbull had conducted a chemical analysis of the stomach contents and had discovered arsenic in sufficient quantity to cause death. They found no other symptom that might indicate disease. The heart was healthy and sound. The inquest was adjourned for another week, but in the meantime Christina Gregg and Edmund Langstreth were arrested and placed in custody on suspicion of murder.

When the inquest resumed, Langstreth was cautioned and questioned about the events of 11 October. He also put in a written statement, denying any knowledge of an attempt on Gregg's life, but admitting 'a criminal intimacy' with Mrs Gregg. John Ferguson was questioned closely, along with several neighbours who said there was bad feeling between the husband and wife. Arthur Bayfield, a chemist, said he had sold some arsenic to someone from Christchurch a few months ago, but could not recollect the man or the circumstances. Peter Cameron, landlord of the Robin Hood Hotel, said Gregg had told him two months ago that he suffered very much from a pain in his insides, and that he believed 'his missus' had given him 'something wrong'.

The inquest jury returned a charge of wilful murder against Christina Gregg, who was removed to the Lyttelton Gaol to await trial before the Supreme Court. Though not included in the verdict, Langstreth was also held in custody.

The Riccarton murder trial, Mr Justice Gresson's first, opened in the Supreme Court in Christchurch on 5 December 1859, and it occupied five days. First of all, the evidence presented at the inquest was repeated for the benefit of the jury. John Ferguson was again questioned closely, and some new details emerged. He said that when he heard Dr Fisher had taken the stomach away he told his sister there would probably be an inquest. She did not seem troubled by this and when he said that it sounded as if Gregg had been poisoned she said at once, 'Well, I don't know whether he has or not.' Ferguson then said, 'You surely know something of it,' but she lifted up her hands and said, 'I declare to God I know nothing of it.' She had asked her husband what he had been drinking at the White Hart before he came home, and he said it was beer. She then said, 'God only knows; probably he might have got it from that, if he has been poisoned.' She would welcome an inquest: she would like to know if her husband had been poisoned, and who had done it.

According to Ferguson, his sister had told him several times over the previous 18 months that Dr Fisher had told James Gregg 'his inside was gone' and he may not have long to live. Gregg's health had declined, and he had moved to stay with his brother-in-law for a few days, so as to be nearer the doctor: 'He seemed low spirited.' Ferguson also said that about three weeks before his death Gregg had told his wife that he could get poison or strychnine whenever he wanted from a boy named Tommy, who had been at Barnard's the auctioneer. Ferguson was not often at his sister's house, but when he did visit, he 'never observed any unhappiness between them'. About six months before she had complained to her brother about Gregg's drinking, and his wasting so much money on alcohol.

Under cross-examination Ferguson admitted, 'after considerable hesitation and consideration', that on the day of Gregg's death he had said in front of Langstreth that he shouldn't wonder if Gregg had poisoned himself, as he had probably bought more land on Banks Peninsula than he could afford to pay for.

Dr Fisher told the court in some detail about the events of 11 October, as he had witnessed them, and about his analysis of the stomach contents with Dr Turnbull. He denied that Gregg had heart disease, or that he had ever said so to Gregg: 'I am of opinion that Gregg must have taken arsenic at the time he was staying at Ferguson's; that his suffering was caused by a dose of arsenic not sufficient to destroy life, but enough to cause great irritation.' He did not think Gregg was the sort of man likely to commit suicide.

The lad generally known as Tom or Tommy, who worked for Barnard, was identified as Thomas Martin. He contradicted Ferguson's testimony, saying that Gregg had never asked him about poison; nor was there any poison kept at Barnard's. Mary Ann Harrington, one of the neighbours, testified that Gregg had been unwell on the Monday, and Mrs Gregg had tried to dissuade him from going to town, but he insisted. When he got ill during the night he asked for water, and said he felt as if he could drink a pail full. Mrs Gregg had told her that he complained a great deal of cramp in his legs and back. Edward Ashby, a miller from Lower Lincoln Road, had been drinking ale with Gregg at the White Hart on the afternoon before his death. Ashby had suffered no ill-effects from what he drank: 'We made business arrangements together. We ought to have been this present week in Pigeon Bay together.'

In his address to the jury, defence counsel James Wyatt drew their attention to the demeanour of Edmund Langstreth: 'The evidence he was giving was on a subject degrading to himself, yet he spoke deliberately and coolly, and exhibited no marks of distress or shame.' When the prisoner suggested she was with child by him, and that she was fearful of her husband's finding out, he replied, 'I said she might do as well as she could.' Wyatt added, 'I noticed the malicious smile of the witness at this stage of his evidence – a smile of which he ought to have been ashamed. Gentlemen, I say that if there is anything in the charge against the prisoner, that witness ought now to be beside her in the dock.'

Wyatt pointed out that all of the evidence was circumstantial, 'and circumstantial evidence not of the best kind'. Though sometimes useful, it was dangerous to rely on it entirely. Most of the witnesses had been women, repeating remarks made at various times in various conversations. Several had contradicted one another.

Wyatt conceded that there was no question about the cause of death: Gregg had died from arsenic poisoning. 'But, gentlemen, I have all through this trial expected to see placed in that box a witness who would swear to having given or sold the prisoner arsenic. But no such witness has been produced. I was astonished. Supposing then the evidence given to have been circumstantial evidence of the very best kind, here was the chief link still wanting.' This was the weak point of the prosecution's case: 'Does anyone suppose that the fact of purchasing arsenic by the prisoner would not have become generally known in a small community like ours, especially when it is considered that all the facts of this case have been before the public for more than a month?'

Wyatt warned the jury that they should pause before passing a verdict on which a person's life might depend, when so much of the evidence was deficient. Dr Fisher had said that Gregg was not a likely person to commit suicide, but 'how is it known that he did not himself commit this act?' Suicides were sometimes committed by people who had shown no previous tendency to do so, and just such a case had occurred not many months ago 'within a few yards from where we are now sitting'. Wyatt concluded his address by stressing that there was 'no proof. A link is wanting. The evidence is purely circumstantial.' It was, he reminded the jury, 'far better that 99 guilty persons should escape than that one innocent person should suffer'.

In summing up, Mr Justice Gresson admitted the possibility of suicide, but made it clear he thought this an unlikely supposition. The most important evidence had been given by Langstreth and Ferguson, and he went over their points at some length. It was clear that Gregg suspected he had been poisoned, and wanted his vomit reserved for the doctor's inspection, but his wife had not kept any of it. He left the decision in the jury's hands: 'It is your duty to take the law from the judge and the facts from the evidence.'

After only half an hour the jury returned and delivered a verdict of not guilty. Christina Gregg was discharged, and supported out of court by her brother and friends. But because this verdict contradicted that of the coroner she was arraigned again, pleading not guilty. Wyatt argued autrefois acquit (previously acquitted), and she was discharged once more.

Despite all the publicity surrounding this case, Christina Gregg continued to live on the family farm and, three years later, on 14 December 1862, she married Edmund Langstreth at St Peter's Church, Upper Riccarton. He was 20 years her junior. According to James Gregg's will, his estate was to pass to his son on Christina's death or remarriage. Yet the couple continued to farm successfully, and bought a further 500 acres of land at Templeton. Eventually young James Gregg took a case to court against his mother and stepfather, seeking the profits they had made since their marriage. Langstreth sold enough land to pay James £750. This transaction may have soured the marriage, or perhaps Langstreth had tired of his older wife, for he had left her by 1880 and returned to England. She continued running the farm at Riccarton until her death in 1882, whereupon Langstreth remarried. He never returned to New Zealand.

In *Poison: The coward's weapon*, David Gee has suggested that the beer at the White Hart might hold the answer to James Gregg's sudden illness and death, but since none of the other patrons fell ill, especially Gregg's drinking companion Edward Ashby, this explanation seems unlikely. Though poison is usually regarded as the coward's weapon for murder, or a woman's preferred weapon, male poisoners are not unknown, and Wyatt seems to have had a strong suspicion that the real culprit was the lover rather than the adulterous wife. The fact that Christina Gregg remained in Riccarton for the rest of her life, and eventually married her lover, regardless of gossip, suggests either that she was innocent of any complicity in her husband's death, or that they were an exceptionally strong-minded and brazen pair of conspirators.

CHAPTER FOUR

THE BROTHEL-KEEPING POLICEMAN

Martin Cash (1808?– 1877), 'the Robin Hood of Van Diemen's land': convict, police constable, bushranger, brothel-keeper, farmer. He shot a constable in Hobart in 1843 while resisting arrest, and spent 10 years on Norfolk Island before receiving a conditional pardon in 1856. After his brief but spectacular career in New Zealand he bought a farm at Glenorchy near Hobart, where he spent the rest of his life.

National Library of Australia, 3290545

Within its first decade Christchurch had become a well-established colonial town, with shops and offices, mostly in wood, and a sprinkling of warehouses, foundries, brickworks and breweries. According to the December 1861 census, Lyttelton was home to about 1900 residents but Christchurch had 3205. The largest occupational category was that of labourer, at 299, closely followed by domestic servant, at 289. The town had 52 clerks and accountants, 153 carpenters and builders, 27 teachers, 12 lawyers, 14 clergymen and 12 medical practitioners. There were 12 brewers and 21 publicans catering for the needs of the thirsty.

Two categories not listed in the census were those of prostitute and brothelkeeper, but there were more than a few of both in 1860s Christchurch. There was a typically colonial imbalance in the gender ratio, with far more single males than females. According to the 1858 census, females made up only 36 per cent of the adult population, and emigration agents were instructed to encourage young single women to come to Canterbury as domestic servants, and then, provided they were 'of good character', to marry and have children. Inevitably, in a raw colonial settlement, there was a minority of so-called 'loose women' who were definitely not of 'good character'.

The police conducted regular surveys of 'houses of ill fame' in Christchurch between 1864 and 1869 and found that the numbers fluctuated, rising when the economy sagged. In March 1864 Inspector Peter Pender claimed there were only 10 known prostitutes working the streets of Christchurch, and that the town was the 'most moral and orderly' he had ever witnessed. By December 1867, however, the number of prostitutes had soared to 39, five of whom had no fixed place of abode. The rest were living in 23 houses of ill fame. They included a mother and daughter team, Elizabeth and Alice King, in Windmill Road (later Antigua Street) on what was then the edge of Sydenham. In several instances prostitutes were still living with their husbands. When a man was out of work, some women were willing to 'go on the game' for a short while to provide an income for the household. Lyttelton, of course, had had its loose women since before the arrival of the First Four Ships. The two most notorious in Christchurch were Eliza Lambert and Mary Ann Robinson. Unlike most of the prostitutes, who plied their trade quietly and discreetly, Lambert was described by police as 'bold and offensive', with seven convictions to her name.

As the population of Christchurch grew, Seager had been urging relocation of the police headquarters from Lyttelton to Christchurch, and the provision of a proper lockup. Tenders were called for a new lockup in April 1858, and Isaac Luck built it, celebrating with a champagne party for his friends. He also built the two-storey police headquarters and barracks alongside the gaol in the Market Place, near the public works office and yard of the provincial government. Luck had earlier built the town's first post office on Colombo Street, facing the pound. With a spacious new market hall also being built (later converted into the chief post office), the Market Place was fast becoming the official and commercial hub of early Christchurch. Seager finally moved his headquarters from Lyttelton to the new building in the Market Place in June 1859.

Seager found it difficult to recruit enough suitable men as constables, so in 1859 he was happy to sign up a new arrival who said he had been a constable in Tasmania. That, however, was not all he had been. Martin Cash was a tall, strong man with red hair and sloping shoulders, a broad chest and powerful hands. He arrived at Lyttelton with a woman presumed to be his wife, and their young child, whom Cash carried on his back. Though his wife was later described as a 'repulsive-looking' hard-faced ex-convict with a 'loud tongue', Cash was well-spoken, suave and charming towards women, with an air of natural authority. Seager had him sworn in as a constable at Christchurch soon after his arrival.

The other constables found Martin Cash an unusual colleague. He said very little and was often absent, as he did not live in the police barracks with the single men. His best mate was the notoriously avaricious Constable Jack Price, who was dismissed from the force in 1860. When a man called Fleetwood committed suicide, they appropriated his new suit. It was too small for Cash, but Price wore it quite brazenly around town on his days off. Cash always seemed to have plenty of money to spend, and soon bought a house in Salisbury Street, just north of the Market Place. Growing suspicious, his colleagues began to follow him and soon discovered that he was not only very familiar with the town's known prostitutes, but seemed to have organised their operation and be taking a percentage of their earnings.[1]

Some of his neighbours in Salisbury Street objected to his

activities and, with the evidence gathered by his fellow police constables, a formal complaint was lodged with Seager and the provincial superintendent. At a special court held in the provincial government offices on 30 March 1860, Cash was found guilty of 'gross misconduct and violation of the regulations, more particularly in harbouring girls of notoriously bad fame at his house in Salisbury Street'. The *Lyttelton Times* loftily remarked that it was 'unnecessary to publish the details', probably because the whole town had by now heard the whispered rumours about the conduct and morality of the Christchurch police force. Martin Cash was fined £5 and dismissed from the force on 2 April 1860, but he had already left on the *Prince Alfred* for Wellington on 31 March.

His previous history now began to emerge. He was brought up in a wealthy family in County Wexford, Ireland, and had a good education, but he shot at a man in a jealous rage for making advances to his sweetheart, and was then sentenced to seven years' transportation for housebreaking. He had arrived in Sydney in 1828 and served his time, earning his ticket of leave and working as a stockman in New South Wales, before settling with another ex-convict, Bessie Clifford. When he was suspected of cattle rustling they decamped to Tasmania, where Cash was caught stealing from an employer. He was again sentenced to seven years, briefly escaped, and had another 18 months added to his sentence. Once again he escaped, and made it across Bass Strait with Bessie, but was caught and sentenced to 10 years at Port Arthur, Tasmania's supposedly escape-proof maximum security prison.[2]

Here he made several breakout attempts, once swimming through shark-infested waters, until in 1842 he successfully escaped with two other convicts. They then embarked on a 20-month spree as bushrangers, robbing mail coaches and homesteads. In 1843, however, Cash heard that his Bessie was living with another man in Hobart, and he swore to kill both of them. In Hobart he was recognised by the police, and a constable was killed in the ensuing gunfight. Cash was sentenced to death by hanging, but was given a last-minute reprieve and transported to Norfolk Island instead. Over the next few years he was a model prisoner, becoming a supervisor and then a constable. Back in Hobart between 1854 and 1856 he was an overseer in the Royal Botanical Gardens, married and had a daughter called Monique. Then in 1859 he and his family came to Lyttelton.

Cash had had a busy day on 30 March 1860, for as well as the special court in the provincial government offices he was also in the Magistrate's Court that day to answer a charge of threatened assault. George Merson stated that as he passed Cash's house the previous Thursday Cash had come out and threatened him, saying 'If I get hold of you, I will give you such a grip as you won't get over!' Merson had at once called a constable and taken him to Cash's house, whereupon Cash had re-emerged and challenged Merson to fight, threatening to 'send him to hell headlong'. Corporal Eldridge bore witness to this exchange. In his own defence, Cash said he had merely wanted to 'have a "round" with Merson to see which was the best man'. He told the court that 'he had got among people who did not appreciate him, and that he intended to leave as soon as he could sell his house'.

The resident magistrate, William John Warburton Hamilton, who had also recently been appointed commissioner of police, told Cash that the law did not permit him to have 'rounds' with people whenever he liked, and bound him to keep the peace for six months on bail of £50, with two sureties for the same amount.

What had been going on between Cash and Merson? Was Merson perhaps one of the neighbours who had objected to having a brothel in their midst?

Cash was not alone in keeping a brothel in the early 1860s. In March 1861 James Evans pleaded guilty to a charge of 'keeping a disorderly and improper house', and to a charge of assault on the premises. His wife Anne pleaded not guilty, saying she had often tried to persuade him to give up their little 'business'. She was acquitted, but the judge gave her 'a severe lecture' and pointed out the consequences if she were to infringe the law again, now that it had been fully explained to her. The assault had occurred when a man named Benjamin Moss went to the Evans house to meet someone, who did not turn up. While waiting, Moss bought a bottle of wine and 'treated' the men and women there:

> Refusing to pay for more wine, he was ordered out of the house, followed by Evans, who knocked him down with a stick, and while on the ground was beaten with a piece of firewood by the female prisoner Taylor, and ultimately removed to the police station in a state of insensibility. Evidence was taken as to the character of the house, but all of it is unfit for publication.

Evans was sentenced to two years' imprisonment with hard labour, in addition to a month for the assault on Moss. Mr Justice Gresson, 'with considerable feeling', addressed the prisoner, pointing out to him 'the fearful and blighting consequences to the community at large which resulted from the traffic [he] had embarked on'.

The prostitutes of Christchurch sometimes made a nuisance of themselves in other ways than by soliciting on the streets. On 26 December 1860 one of the more flamboyant ladies of the night, Catherine Fleetwood, decided she would like to attend the theatre with a group of her fellow workers, but the manager refused to let them in. They collected opposite the theatre in High Street and 'commenced singing and dancing, and using most improper language, to the great annoyance of passers by'. They were ordered away, but kept coming back. Attracted by the noise, a large number of men and boys collected, blocking the footpath. Fleetwood's language was described as 'very bad, she being under the influence of drink at the time'. The *Lyttelton Times* noted that these women were among those who had came out to Canterbury on the *Mystery* the previous year, with strong recommendations from Lord Shaftesbury and 'the matrons of certain reformatory schools'. It would appear that some of these 'fallen women' had returned to their former ways – and continued to do so. Fleetwood was in court again in April 1862, on an obscene language charge.

Martin Cash did not disappear, as Seager probably hoped he would. He was soon back in Christchurch, once again operating brothels in various houses north of Cathedral Square. The most notorious was the 'Red House' in Salisbury Street, near St Luke's Church, on the way to the Barbadoes Street cemetery, which was itself notorious as a place for illicit coupling after dark. Cash was now careful to avoid any personal involvement in crime. It has been suggested that he became something of a 'godfather' figure, organising the brothels and taking a cut from their proceeds, but staying in the background. Another of his notorious houses in the 1860s was 'the White House' in Peterborough Street. One of his former 'girls', Emma Craigie, was often in court, however, involved in assault or disorderly conduct cases. In July 1861 she appeared as a witness for Emma Bennett, who had been assaulted by one Richard Offwood. Having stated that she lived at Mrs Craigie's in Armagh Street, Emma Bennett described how, on 27 June, Offwood

> came into the house and asked for a bed, and he asked her to sleep with him; she refused, and he was going to strike her, and swept all the articles off the mantel-piece; he had an open penknife in one hand and a broken vase in the other; she held the hand he had the knife in, and in the scuffle she got cut in the hand, but whether it was by the knife or the vase she could not state; a policeman was sent for and the prisoner was removed.

Under questioning Emma Bennett admitted that they had all been drinking, and that she had sent out for the drink:

> I have been living a long time with Mrs. Craigie; she provides me a bedroom; I am not in service with her. Mr. Martin keeps me and the child; he pays for board and lodging for me. Mrs. Craigie is kept by Mr. Hart; she rents the house; the house is a brothel; I was only slightly hurt.

Emma Bennett now decided she did not want to press the charge against Offwood, and the magistrate ordered him to be discharged.

The very next case that day was against the notorious prostitute Eliza Lambert, who was charged with using 'profane and obscene language in Armagh Street, Christchurch', on 27 July. She was fined 10s, with 4s in costs.

Prostitutes rarely had that sort of money to spare, and their usual fate was to spend a week in the lockup in the Market Place instead, unless their madam or the man who kept them was willing to pay the fine and offset it against their future earnings. Emma Craigie was back in court on 30 August 1862 charged with disorderly conduct in one of Cash's brothels. Ordered to keep the peace for 12 months, she was unable to find the surety and spent time in prison.

It must have been deeply embarrassing for Seager and his constables to see Martin Cash walking about as a free man and running a string of brothels. Two constables, Alfred Missen and George Bannerman, together with the police station cook, Richard Rumble, could stand this no longer, and in October 1862 they took matters into their own hands. After midnight on 8 October they knocked at the back door of the 'Red House' in Salisbury Street and when it was opened they forced their way in. Catherine Fleetwood and Fanny Harding told them to leave but they refused. Cash appeared and laid hands on Rumble to throw him out, but Rumble punched Cash and knocked him down. Cash got up but Rumble struck him again, this time with something hard, perhaps a bottle. Missen and Bannerman took Rumble back to the police station, with Cash following them, bleeding from a head wound. On his arrival at the police station Cash collapsed and had to be carried back to the 'Red House' on a stretcher. A doctor was called, who declared the wound 'quite serious'.

The court hearing was adjourned until 3 December so that Cash could recover from his injuries, but the grand jury threw out the charge against Rumble. The evidence of two prostitutes and a notorious ex-convict was not thought sufficient to send the case to trial.

Pressure on the police from the respectable elite of Christchurch to do something about Cash and his brothels appears to have mounted throughout 1862. Another incident at the 'White House' on 15 November added to the outrage. Mary Younghusband was one of the prostitutes working there with Mary Ann Robinson, and John Heron was among a group of men drinking there that night. About daybreak Heron burst into Younghusband's bedroom and told her he wanted to sleep with her. She refused, and struggled to stop Heron from climbing into bed with her. She claimed that he used abusive language and hit her on the head with a bottle, which caused a 3in (7.5cm) wound, open to the bone. One of Heron's friends, Robert McMahon, said she was very drunk at the time and got the wound by falling over onto a bottle. The jury in the Supreme Court on 3 December doubted the prostitute's evidence, and found Heron not guilty.

Just before Heron's trial a warrant was issued for the arrest of Martin Cash for keeping a 'bawdy house and disorderly house'. The charge is worth quoting in full as an example of the breathless legal prose of the day. Cash was alleged to have kept

> a certain Common Bawdy house situated in Peterborough Street in the said city and unlawfully and wickedly did keep and maintain in the said house divers evil disposed persons as well as men and women and whores on the days and times aforesaid as well as in the night as in the day there unlawfully and wickedly did receive and entertain and in which said house the said evil disposed persons and whores by the consent and procurement of the said Martin Cash on the days and times aforesaid there did commit whoredom and fornication whereby divers unlawful assemblies, riots, routs, affrays, disturbances and violations of the peace of Our Lady the Queen and dreadful and lewd offences [took place] in the same house.

Cash appeared in court on 10 March 1863 and was convicted as charged, but a deal was struck. His lawyer, the splendidly named Fitzgerald Herbert Ruxton Caffey, was back in court the following day asking the Supreme Court to have him released and his £200 surety returned to him. The motion was allowed after the court had been assured that the 'Red House' had been sold and Cash had promised to leave the city.

Martin Cash went to try his luck on the Otago goldfields and did fairly well, or so he later claimed. He got into trouble with the law there, too, and briefly returned to Christchurch to withdraw his ill-gotten gains – allegedly some £2000 – from the bank, and sailed back to Tasmania. There he bought a farm at Glenorchy and settled down with his wife and children. Late in life he told the story of his colourful career to James Lester Burke, who edited and published it in 1870 as *The Adventures of Martin Cash*. Cash died in his bed in 1877, one of Australia's most celebrated bushrangers and remembered in New Zealand as 'the greatest scoundrel of whom there is any record in Canterbury'.[3]

CHAPTER FIVE

RAPES, STABBINGS AND INDECENT ASSAULT

Christchurch's first police barracks and lockup [4], built by Isaac Luck in 1858, in the Market Place (later renamed Victoria Square). At left are the Public Works yard and office of the Canterbury Provincial Government, and at right the immigration barracks [5] (later converted into the first fire station). Behind them is Colombo Street [3].

Brittenden collection

T he 1860s saw Christchurch mature rapidly as the chief market town for the settlers of the Canterbury Plains. Banks appeared in both Lyttelton and Christchurch in 1861 and 1862 to serve the increasing numbers of retailers and merchants, and communications improved with the opening of the first telegraph line in New Zealand between port and town in July 1862. The provincial government borrowed heavily for Canterbury's most ambitious but most urgent engineering project, a railway line between port and town that would pass under the Port Hills through a tunnel starting in the Heathcote Valley. The first part of this broad-gauge line, linking Christchurch to the wharf at Ferrymead, was opened in December 1863 with Canterbury's first steam locomotive, *Pilgrim*. The tunnel took four years to complete, opening in December 1867, and it proved the making of the local economy, enabling heavy goods to pass easily to and from Lyttelton. It was as if Canterbury now had its 'throat' and could breathe deeply. Increasing exports of wool and grain soon made the province wealthy, while land sales filled the coffers of the provincial government.

Migrants continued to arrive in large numbers during the 1860s, the largest ship of this period, *British Empire*, bringing 574 migrants on one voyage in September 1864. But not all the new arrivals stayed in Canterbury. The 1860s were also the decade of major gold rushes, to Otago in 1861 and the West Coast in 1865. Westland was then part of Canterbury Province, and the newspapers at first talked hopefully of the 'West Canterbury goldfield', but most of the gold went across the Tasman Sea to Australia, and Christchurch never enjoyed the spectacular prosperity that Dunedin won from Otago's gold. Many of Christchurch's young single men, and not a few married ones as well, joined the rush to the West Coast to make their fortunes, only to return after a year or two, a few better off but many more disappointed. The gold attracted miners from Australia and even California, making Lyttelton and Christchurch staging posts to the diggings. The city suddenly acquired a floating population of itinerant men, which raised fears among the respectable about an influx of riff-raff and criminals, and what they might do while in town.

Crime certainly increased in Christchurch during the early 1860s, but this was largely because the town's population was also rising rapidly, topping 7000 in 1866. That year saw the province's population reach 58,752, with only 31 per cent of that total being female. Jeremy Finn's research has revealed that the number of cases appearing before the Supreme Court in Canterbury peaked at 90 in 1865, dropping away to less than 30 in 1871. The ratio of cases per 1000 of population remained comparatively low, fluctuating across the 1860s to drop from two in 1860 to 0.6 in 1871. The total number of convictions from cases committed to the Supreme Court between 1852 and 1872 was 497, giving a conviction rate for Canterbury of 74 per cent, well above the New Zealand rate of 65 per cent.

Sexual offending in Lyttelton and Christchurch also rose dramatically in this decade, with more cases in the one year of 1867 than were heard in the whole of the 1850s. The newspapers commented on the increase, noting that sexual assaults had been rare in the settlement before then, but their refusal to publish details of the court proceedings makes it difficult to assess the role of juries in acquitting or convicting in such cases.

William McDonald appeared in court to face a charge of raping Martha Stupple in 1862, and the Press reported his acquittal in a tone of disapproval:

> The charge was sustained by the evidence of the prosecutrix, of a young man named [Edward] Withers, and a labourer who assisted in taking the prisoner to the police barracks, but though their evidence appeared conclusive against the prisoner the jury, after three hours' consideration, returned a verdict of not guilty, apparently as much to the surprise of the prisoner as it evidently was to everyone present who heard the evidence.

The first conviction for rape in the Christchurch Supreme Court was that of Jacob Small in June 1862. He was not known to the victim, and he was an outsider, described as a 'man of colour', probably of African ancestry. As he was considered a 'foreigner', Mr Justice Gresson appointed counsel to represent him. Though the evidence was circumstantial it was enough to convince the jury. Small had broken into the victim's house at night and had left distinctive footprints that could be matched to his boots.

Robert Fisher's case in June 1864 attracted considerably more publicity. He was accused of raping the wife of a fellow farm worker, and though the defence attempted to portray the wife as an immoral woman who had initiated the sexual activity, the jury declared him guilty. The victim's husband had accepted £30 (about $3000 today) from the accused as compensation for the injury to his wife.

It is safe to assume that many rapes and sexual assaults were, then as now, not reported to the police. Some cases came to court but failed when the victim did not turn up to testify against her assailant. Sometimes they failed even when the victim did turn up. In September 1864 Daniel Buckley was charged with assault with intent to commit the rape of Mrs Elizabeth Wilson of Lake Ellesmere, but she was unable to get to court because of the flooded Selwyn River. He was remanded with two sureties of £500 each until the following week, when she was able to travel to Christchurch. However, 'after hearing the evidence, which was unfit for publication, the case was dismissed'.

One of the few sexual cases to be reported at length in the 1860s was that of James O'Kelly, who was convicted of 'carnally knowing a girl under the age of twelve'. (The age of consent remained 12 until 1893, when it was raised to 14. It became 16 in 1896.) Elizabeth Judson had been a servant in his house in 1861, had been seduced by him and gave birth to a child shortly after her twelfth birthday. The *Lyttelton Times* described her as an 'interesting, precocious-looking girl'. O'Kelly, who was 57, said that she had not told him her age at the time. He also claimed that Judson had fabricated her evidence to extort money, and that the child was not his. Mr Justice Gresson pointed out, however, that a mistaken belief about her age was no defence in law, and did not reduce the accused's moral guilt. He was sentenced to six months in prison with hard labour.

An unusual case in March 1869 led to a punishment that would be regarded as barbaric today. Henry Laurence, a boy not yet 14, pleaded guilty to a charge of indecent assault. His defence counsel said he was very repentant and could provide evidence of good character, but Mr Justice Gresson took a stern view: 'The depositions show a most wanton and grievous outrage has been committed on a young girl on a Sunday, as she was sitting and reading her Bible close to her father's house. I cannot conceive a more wanton outrage than has been committed in this case.'

Defence counsel raised the possibility of corporal punishment to reduce the prison sentence, and Gresson agreed. He was opposed to corporal punishment in general because it was degrading for adults, 'but for youth and for a class of offences of this nature I think it is a particularly suitable punishment'. Laurence was sentenced to one month in prison with hard labour and two whippings of 12 lashings each with the cat o' nine tails.

Victorian moral standards were notoriously strict, and Victorian prudery has become legendary, even though much hypocrisy was to be found in the private lives of public figures. A woman's glimpse of a man's penis as he urinated in a side alley could end in court with a charge of indecent exposure in a public place. Nudity was to be shunned lest it arouse improper thoughts or lustful urges. Yet most men bathed naked in the early nineteenth century if they thought there were no women in the vicinity. At Oxford University in England there was a stretch of the river reserved for male bathing at certain times of the day, and women were warned not to go there. On one famous occasion a boatload of women passed that part of the riverbank by mistake and startled a number of naked male bathers, most of whom hastily concealed their private parts. The cleverest of them, however, held his hat over his face.

In January 1865 Thomas Priest appeared in the Lyttelton Magistrate's Court before Dr Donald and JPs William John Warburton Hamilton, Hugh Murray-Aynsley and Robert Rhodes to answer a charge of nude bathing within view of a public road. The information had been laid by Constable George Bannerman, at the request of Hamilton, whose house overlooked the bathing beach in Dampiers Bay. Bannerman said he had gone to the bathing place for a dip on Saturday 16 January and there saw Priest and two other men bathing. After he had dried and dressed himself, a messenger came from Hamilton's house to ask who the other bathers were. Hamilton then asked him to lay a complaint. The constable said he was wearing drawers himself, but had not noticed whether the others were. The bathing shed was in view of the public road, but at a distance of about 100 yards: 'He could be seen from Mr. Hamilton's residence if anyone looked purposely.'

The defence called Lyttelton stationer and bookseller E. Mills, who had been on the committee that had selected the beach as a municipal bathing place. He did not consider it indecent to bathe there since it was a good distance from the public road: 'It would be difficult to tell the sex of any one at that distance without glasses.' In his own defence Priest said he had bathed according to the regulations, the man in charge of the bathing shed never told him it was necessary to wear drawers, and as a resident of the town he felt entitled to swim there. The court was cleared, and after half an hour's discussion the bench was unanimously of the opinion that the charge could not be sustained, as no act of indecency was proven. The *Press* report concluded: 'The Court was densely crowded, and the decision of the Bench appeared to give great satisfaction.'

Crimes of violence in this period rarely involved firearms, but knives were much in evidence, with a dozen stabbings in the 1860s. One assault involved a sword-stick, another a military sword. The latter was a case of self-defence against a burglar. A lawyer living in Lyttelton, Robert D'Oyly, was woken one morning in August 1864 by the sound of someone breaking a lock and entering his house. He was alone, so he armed himself with a sword before proceeding downstairs with his weapon in one hand a candle in the other. He found a man later identified as Samuel McCarthy hiding behind a door. D'Oyly ordered him to stand still or be run through. The man remained quiet at first, but when D'Oyly shouted 'Police! Thieves!' he rushed at D'Oyly, knocking him backwards over an empty case.

D'Oyly struck at McCarthy's face and inflicted deep wounds on his temple and nose.

McCarthy then fell on him and tried to get hold of the sword, but D'Oyly kept a tight hold of the handle and stabbed him in the side. McCarthy fainted from loss of blood and fell insensible to the floor. D'Oyly kept shouting for assistance, and two men named Burns and Toomey arrived, followed some minutes later by the police. A *Press* reporter had also heard the noise and came to the door to see McCarthy lying on his back with 'fearful wounds on his face and temples (the nose being completely divided), from which blood was issuing very profusely'. A stretcher was found and McCarthy was taken to the police barracks where Dr John Rouse and Dr Donald sewed up his wounds.

Next morning the Magistrate's Court heard that McCarthy was the former master of the schooner *Thetis*, and had been working lately on the steamer *Eleanor*. Toomey testified that McCarthy had visited his house the previous night, and had 'talked in such a rambling style as to lead to the conclusion that he was not right in his head'. Having persuaded him to stay the night, Toomey sat up with him for some hours. But McCarthy suddenly got up and rushed out of the house, down Oxford Street and around the Queen's Hotel into London Street. Toomey and Burns had followed him but lost him there, until they heard the shouts for help coming from D'Oyly's place. Toomey said that McCarthy had been drinking hard for the previous two weeks, and feared he was suffering from delirium tremens.

Dr Rouse testified that McCarthy had a flesh wound over his ribs on one side, a severe cut down the temple and nose, which was divided downwards, and cuts on the cheek. He was also 'suffering from the effects of hard drinking'. While waiting for McCarthy to recover to face a charge of breaking and entering, D'Oyly wrote a letter to the *Press*, deploring the prevalence of drunkenness in Canterbury. He blamed the legislators, claiming that the provincial government's ordinance against tippling was a dead letter because nobody was willing to enforce it. McCarthy does not appear to have pressed charges over his injuries. He may have been advised that he was lucky to be alive, and that a Christchurch jury would have shown little sympathy for a burglar caught in the act.

D'Oyly had a valid point. The Magistrate's Court reports of the 1860s are full of drunken and disorderly cases. Some names recur, especially those of known prostitutes such as Emma Craigie. In October 1864 she was released from gaol after serving 12 months in prison with hard labour, only to be arrested for being drunk and disorderly a few days later. She had also been using abusive language in a public place: 'Prisoner was very riotous in Court, and the Resident Magistrate ordered her to be bound over to be of good behaviour, on her own recognizance of £100 [about $10,000] and two sureties in £100 each.' Unable to find such a sum, or anyone to put up a surety, she went straight back to prison.

Just the month before, a girl called Minnie, 'one of the unfortunates in Christchurch' (a euphemism for a prostitute), was charged with attempted suicide by taking poison and jumping into the Avon River: 'It appeared that this unfortunate girl had been in a good situation, but had been led astray into taking to the course of life which she has been carrying on.' She was remanded while enquiries were made, probably to contact her family. Single girls who emigrated to Canterbury with no family to support them were terribly vulnerable to loneliness and alcohol and were easily taken advantage of.

Those who succumbed to depression and alcohol were likely to finish up in the new lunatic asylum in Lincoln Road, hopefully named Sunnyside after a famous asylum in Scotland. The first patients were admitted to Sunnyside in December 1863, under the kindly care of former police sub-inspector Edward Seager, who was the first steward at Sunnyside; his wife Esther was its first matron. Together they created the most humane and advanced mental asylum for its time in the southern hemisphere. There was no resident medical officer, but Seager's reputation, and his charm, ensured the cooperation of Christchurch's small medical fraternity. A practical man, he wanted to make Sunnyside self-supporting, with its own farm. Good food, fresh air, company and occupational therapy, though the term had not yet been invented, were the simple and effective treatments he adopted. Seager was convinced that alcohol was a major factor in the rising incidence of both crime and mental illness in the settlement, and could support his case from the Lyttelton Gaol admission books (which sadly no longer exist). Some of his 'cures' over the next few years probably included depressed alcoholics who had been given the opportunity to dry out.

Seager, Magistrate Christopher Bowen and Mr Justice Gresson were all agreed on the need for a juvenile reformatory in Canterbury, so that young offenders were not locked up with hardened criminals and thus condemned to crime as a way of life. One sad case in 1865 demonstrated this problem. On 29 May, Mary Ann Greaves, one of the city's notorious prostitutes, appeared before Bowen in the Magistrate's Court charged with keeping a brothel 'and otherwise misbehaving herself'. She was sent to prison, as she could not find the sureties for good behaviour. Then her 12-year-old daughter Catherine was brought up on a charge of stealing money in a brothel. Bowen said he had great hesitation in committing a child for trial, but he thought she might be better off in gaol than living with such a mother.

Catherine Greaves was committed for trial at the next session of the Supreme Court, and Mr Justice Gresson told the jurors:

> There is one very distressing case, which illustrates forcibly the
> want of a reformatory, more especially for juvenile offenders and
> females. It is the case of a girl scarcely beyond the age of child-
> hood, trained to a commission of crime by a most abandoned
> mother, who is not restrained even by the presence of her own
> child from indulgence in her vicious habits. For a child so unfor-
> tunately circumstanced, a reformatory, humanely speaking, offers
> the only chance of rescue from utter destruction ... in this case,
> if there should be a conviction, I must assume that the moral
> atmosphere of our gaol, even with all its deplorable deficiencies,
> is less pernicious than the society of such a mother.

The grand jury, however, thought otherwise and found no true bill – insufficient evidence to support the charge – against Catherine Greaves, who was free to go. With her mother in gaol, where did she go? The orphanage was one possible destination, but it is more likely that she went to live with the only friends she knew, her mother's fellow 'sisters of the night'.

Earlier that same year one of her mother's old friends had been in court as a result of trying to see her daughter, or at least a girl she claimed was her daughter. Mary Ann Robinson, 'of painful notoriety', appeared in the Magistrate's Court charged with breaking windows at the Christchurch Orphan Asylum, and using obscene language 'to the annoyance of its inhabitants'. The orphanage secretary/schoolmaster, T. L. Stanley, the matron Mrs Henry and one of the servants gave evidence. They had frequently been troubled by Robinson's visits to see her daughter, but because there was some doubt about whether the girl, who did not want to see her, really was her daughter, she was refused entry. Robinson had come once again on 21 March and, after being denied admittance, started breaking windows and using 'the most disgusting language' outside the building.

Robinson said in her defence that it was strange that she was not allowed to visit her own daughter. She had 'been foolish before, but now she was one of the best-conducted women in the colony', and hoped the magistrate would look favourably on her case. Bowen had seen this repeat offender so often over the years that he probably had difficulty keeping a straight face. He replied that if the child was hers then this was not the way to gain access to her: 'She had a proper course which she could pursue if she chose; she had not done so, and as she was well known in this Court she would be fined £3 with a promise that if she ever appeared again she would be imprisoned without a fine.'

Mary Ann Robinson could not restrain herself, however. As she left the court she made 'some insolent remarks to the matron of the Asylum, to the effect that she would not be long in her place'. Bowen called her back and inflicted a larger fine of £5, with the alternative of 14 days in prison with hard labour. She paid the fine.

Two more old offenders appeared before the resident magistrate early in 1866. Margaret Bowen, aged 35, 'of painful notoriety' (and presumably no relation to the magistrate), was fined £3 for disorderly conduct in Gloucester Street one evening outside the first Theatre Royal. Unable to pay the fine, she was sent to prison for four days. The *Press* noted that the government would now have to provide for four of her young children while she was locked up.

A few days later, Jane Glass, aged 31, another 'old offender', was charged with being drunk and incapable. She had come out of gaol only two days before. She admitted the offence, but asked the magistrate to be lenient, as she intended leaving the colony. Bowen remarked drily that experience had shown it was no use being lenient with her, and fined her £5. Unable to pay, she went back to prison for 14 days.

Assaults and robberies gave occasional light relief from these sad cases of alcoholic prostitutes. In 1866 'a notorious character' named Henry Brown was charged with the assault and robbery of one Peter Scott, a clerk who lived in Peterborough Street. Scott said he did not know Brown, and had never spoken to him before the early morning of 5 February. Having eaten a late supper that did not agree with him, Scott thought he needed some fresh air so he went for a walk towards the Colombo Street bridge. Feeling sick, he sat down at the side of the road. Labourer Edward McCulley, one of Brown's associates, now picks up the story:

> I know Brown's house in Kilmore Street. I was there about two a.m. yesterday. I saw Brown outside the house. I went up the garden with him ... He knocked at his own door, and a woman came to it, and he asked her to give him out that bottle of grog. She gave it to him. He drank some, and passed it to me. I drank some, and he drank the remainder, and he threw the bottle to the ground.

As the pair were heading away from the house McCulley noticed a man lying at the corner of the footpath and said, 'Here is a man drunk.' He lifted him to his feet and asked him who he was. 'He appeared to be sick, and said he could make his own way home. He walked towards Colombo Street.' Brown then said, 'I'll go and kick up a row with him,' but McCulley replied, 'Brown, if you do, you'll get yourself into trouble; the man is drunk and you have no business interfering with him.' At this point the other man returned and he and Brown 'then struck out at each other. When they had made one or two blows I saw fire fly from the stones in the road between the two. I thought there was a weapon, so I walked away ... I cannot say who struck first.'

Frederick Hitches was a neighbour who had no connection with Brown, and may therefore have been a more reliable witness. He was asleep in bed when he heard a cry of 'Murder!':

> When I got outside there were two young women crying murder. I saw two men run past the window, and run in the direction of the Devonshire Arms. I went to the house from where the cries came. I saw a young woman looking out of a window. She said, 'For God's sake, come in, they are murdering this man!' After some delay, she let me in, and she had the toma-hawk ... in her hand. It was smeared with blood. She said, 'There has been two or three men here, beating this man.' I examined him, and found only a slight scratch on the left temple ... When I came in first, Brown was on the floor, and seemed to have his senses about him, but afterwards commenced kicking at the wall and floor. The blood on the tomahawk was running, and warm. I sent for the police.

The woman's name was Phoebe, and it looks as if Brown had given her the weapon and told her to make out that he had been the victim. Constable Robert McKnight was called to the house, where he found Brown 'lying there, apparently in a fit. There was blood on his trousers.' Leaving Constable Wilson in charge, McK-night headed up Colombo Street to Alexander Doran's house. Just behind the building he found 'a pool of blood, at Miss Smith's door. I traced the blood across the fence, behind the school-house.' (This was probably the school at St Luke's Church.) McKnight then went to Scott's house, where there was a pool of blood at the back door. Scott was in bed. 'He had a cut under each eye, a cut at the back of his head, and one across the nose.' Based on what Scott told him, McKnight arrested Brown, who was still lying in what appeared to be a fainting fit. When McKnight ordered Wilson to handcuff him, however, Brown 'became very violent and we had to put him on a truck and tie him to get him to the lockup [in the Market Place]'.

Dr William Deamer, called to attend to Scott, 'found him lying in bed and bleeding profusely. He had a large wound in the scalp down to the bone, and three smaller ones on the face ... He was exhausted, and seemed to have lost a great deal of blood.'

The case was adjourned until Scott was well enough to appear in court. He identified Brown as one of the men who came up to him as he was sitting in the gutter feeling ill:

> I got up and went towards Colombo Street. The men followed me and overtook me, about ten yards from Colombo Street. I was struck a blow in the face. I don't remember anything being said before this. I believe [the] prisoner to be the man who struck me. I was struck with a hammer with a sharp edge ... I attempted to get the hammer from him. We both fell. I got away from him, and went round the corner of Colombo Street. The same man overtook me, and we had another struggle. I got away from him again.

Desperate to escape, Scott turned into Doran's gate, but Brown struck him again several times with the hammer, 'with both the edge and the other side', on the face, head, arms and shoulders. When Scott was on the ground Brown said, 'Now will you give me your bloody money?' Afraid for his life, Scott gave Brown a sovereign, a half-sovereign and some silver, but refused to give up his watch. He fainted and when he came to Brown had gone. 'I bled a great deal. I went home across the gardens.'

Committing Brown for trial in the Supreme Court, Bowen remarked on the cowardly behaviour of McCulley, who had gone home instead of assisting the victim: 'to say the least of it, it was a very un-English-like proceeding'. At the Supreme Court trial held in the town hall in High Street on 3 March Brown had the cheek to plead not guilty, but the witnesses all repeated the same testimony they had given in the lower court. Brown called no witnesses and said he did not wish to say anything. The jury, without retiring, agreed on a guilty verdict, and Mr Justice Gresson sentenced him to three years in prison with hard labour.

Another stabbing case in 1866 underlined the need for a reformatory for juvenile offenders. Henry Hayton, a lad of 13, appeared before Magistrate Bowen on a charge of stabbing with intent. The prosecutor was Joseph Day, who had just been appointed as the pilot at Sumner, the start of a 40-year career that would make him one of the seaside village's best-known residents. His father George had been an overseer for Captain Thomas during the early construction of the Lyttelton–Sumner road, and had then built a hotel. Though its signboard said 'Sumner Hotel', it was known to everyone in Canterbury as Day's.

Apparently the boy Hayton had been giving cheek, and Day had threatened to box his ears. The boy then drew a knife, and when Day went to take it from him the boy struck at him twice, inflicting cuts on his arm. Bowen, at a loss as to what was best for so young an offender, took another day to think about it. He also made some discreet enquiries, so that when Hayton reappeared the next day Bowen could tell the court that the boy was an orphan, had been discarded by all his friends and, after wandering the streets doing nothing, he had ended up using his knife against a respectable citizen. Bowen did not like to send young lads to gaol to mix with hardened criminals, but there was nowhere else to send him. He discharged Hayton, ordering the police to keep a strict eye on him. If he offended again he would certainly be imprisoned. Bowen added that he would be urging the government to set up a reformatory school in Canterbury.

Death by stabbing accounted for a third of all homicides in New Zealand in this period — beatings made up another third — yet in Canterbury all but one of the murder convictions in the 1860s involved stabbing. Knives, swords and bayonets seemed to be the preferred weapons of local murderers. One such case concerned non-Canterbury people, but just happened to occur in Lyttelton. In September 1865 some sailors from the *Rona* had been ashore drinking in one or more of Lyttelton's numerous pubs, and were attempting to return to the ship in a rowing boat. A fight broke out in the stern between a half-caste Fijian named Henri Ives, and an American named Edgar S. Achis (or Ackis). According to their shipmate James Wright Anderson, known as Jim Wright, they were rolling about in the stern sheets, punching and wrestling. At one point Achis cried, 'Jim Wright! Henri has knifed me.' (In the court Ives called out, 'Me no knife Ned. Ned knife me.') In the scuffle an oar was lost overboard, and they had to scull slowly back to the ship with one oar. Along the way Achis asked another sailor, Jim Anderson, to move his leg, so he was still alive at that point. When they reached the *Rona* Ives scrambled up the side of the ship and went straight to his hammock in the forecastle. Achis appeared to be asleep, so the mate rigged a strop and tackle to hoist him aboard. They carried him to the galley and there saw blood on his shirt. Then they realised he was dead.

Ives was charged with wilful murder, but the jury after half an hour returned a verdict of manslaughter. Mr Justice Gresson adjourned the court for a day to consider the sentence. When the court reassembled on 6 December, with Mary Ann Toon interpreting, Ives made a long and tearful statement. He said they had had an argument in the boat, and the American had raised a knife to strike him, but he had managed to wrench it out of his hand and in so doing had stabbed him. Ives then threw the knife and belt into the water. He said they were all very drunk. He had not quarrelled with the American before. In fact, Achis had been 'like a brother' to him, but he knew he was a dangerous man, as he had several previous convictions. Gresson, satisfied that the accused was remorseful, sentenced him to three years in the Lyttelton Gaol with hard labour.

However, sympathetic friends started a petition on Ives' behalf, and on 10 December 1868 he was pardoned and discharged from prison. The Canterbury *Police Gazette* described him as a swarthy Fijian islander with black curly hair and hazel eyes. He was then aged 23 and was 5ft 7in (169cm) tall. He had a heart tattooed on his left arm, and on his right arm his name with a star in red and blue. Ives appears to have settled in Lyttelton and started a family, for he served a month in prison in 1871 for deserting his illegitimate child.

Alcohol was a major theme in many of the court cases in 1860s Christchurch. Some notorious publicans were often before the magistrate to be fined for minor breaches of the licensing laws, usually for selling alcohol outside the prescribed hours. Others, even the more respectable ones, were fined for failing to keep a light burning above their door during the hours of darkness. Publicans also had to be careful not to allow prostitutes to use their premises for soliciting or conducting their business. Two publicans thus charged in January 1866 were let off only because the new Public House Ordinance of 1866 had not yet reached the magistrate, and the police complaints had been laid under the old 1863 ordinance.

Others, of course, attempted to bypass the pubs altogether and make their own liquor. Patrick Gallagher appeared in the Magistrate's Court in September 1866 charged with having a still at his house in Montreal Street, in breach of the Distillation Prohibition Ordinance. Inspector Peter Pender had gone to the house with Mr Rose, the deputy collector of customs, after a tip-off. There they found Gallagher and his wife, and a man named McAllister, who was working on some tin pipe. In the kitchen they removed a piece of carpet to reveal a trapdoor leading to a cellar 7ft deep, 7ft wide and 10ft long (2m x 2m x 3m). Pender went down a ladder and found another brick fireplace in the cellar, with a chimney joined to the kitchen chimney. On one side a pipe brought water from an artesian well, while on the other a drain carried the waste water outside into a small creek. On a table was the 'Tin' or distillation apparatus that was later produced in court. According to Rose, Pender had remarked, 'Here we have got every blessed thing [for making whisky].'

Pender then asked to inspect the outhouse, where he found a number of wooden casks, one of which was full. Gallagher said he was a cooper by trade, then that some men had been using the shed and doing business that he did not like, and he had ordered them away. Pender ignored this feeble attempt at an alibi. Outside was another cask, which Gallagher claimed contained beer. Pender then went into Gallagher's workshop and found another full cask, which Gallagher said he had obtained from Ward's Brewery. But underneath some matting Pender discovered another 'Tin' for distilling. Gallagher, who 'seemed alarmed', said the men must have put it there during the night.

Rose tested the beer in one of the casks, found it was sweet and fermenting and declared it to be 'wash', used for distilling. The beer in the next cask was even sweeter than that in the first. Pender arrested Gallagher and sent for another constable, James Rowley, who came to inspect the cellar. He later told the court that he had attended three or four seizures of illicit stills in Otago, and confirmed that Gallagher's cellar was a purpose-made distilling operation. Defence counsel Dr C. J. Foster, whose father was a brewer, contended that the still was in pieces and not in working order, and therefore could not be called a still, but Bowen said the evidence appeared to be overwhelming. This offence carried a heavy fine, ranging from £100 up to £500 for repeat offences. As Gallagher had no previous convictions, Bowen fined him £100.

One of the few indecent assault cases fully reported in the *Press* in the 1860s was that of Henry Ballinger, who appeared in the Supreme Court charged with an assault on Mrs Mary Ward as she was walking up the Bridle Path from Lyttelton on 4 September 1866. She said that Ballinger had approached her at the foot of the Bridle Path and said 'Good morning', but she did not respond. He walked alongside her up the track, but she told him he was mistaken and was taking a great deal of liberty in talking to her. He claimed to mean no harm. She walked on, and he followed. Two men came down the track towards Lyttelton and Ballinger stopped to talk to them. Mary Ward went on out of sight around a curve, then heard him coming up quickly behind her:

> I turned round; he seized me by the waist with one hand and
> by the neck with the other. He made use of improper language,
> and said he would strangle me. I said I would lay an information
> against him. He said, 'If you make an alarm or lay an information
> against me I will throw you down that precipice.'

Just then, Mary Ward saw a man coming down the Bridle Path and Ballinger ran back towards Lyttelton.

In fact there were two men coming down the track. One was James Wallace, who testified that he saw a man and woman near the top of the Bridle Path, coming up the hill. He recognised them as Mrs Ward and Ballinger. After he had passed he heard a woman scream, and looked back to see Ballinger with his hand on her shoulder. Ballinger then ran down the hill. The other witness was John Faulkner, who also saw Ballinger take off towards Lyttelton. Mrs Ward complained to him that she had been assaulted. Later that day Faulkner saw Ballinger in Lyttelton and spoke to him: 'What have you been doing on the hill?' Ballinger replied, 'What do you mean?' Faulkner said, 'About that woman.' Ballinger said, 'I never touched the woman.' But Faulkner fancied that Ballinger knew the woman, and he did not deny being on the hill. Sergeant Daniel Niall told the court that when he arrested Ballinger the accused had said he walked with Mrs Ward to the top of the hill, but let go of her when she objected.

Lawyer Henry Wynn Williams, conducting Ballinger's defence, called as a witness Letitia Haydon, who lived in Salt's Gully, Lyttelton. Ballinger had been a lodger in her house for a year or more. Mary Ward, who also lived in Salt's Gully, passed her house every day to fetch water. Letitia Haydon had heard Ballinger speak to her many times. He would say, 'My jewel, will I carry the water for you?'

Nelson Haydon said he had known Ballinger for two years, and knew Mrs Ward as a neighbour: 'I have often seen them talking together, walking along the street.' Henry Barker, a carrier, knew Ballinger well: 'I used to go about with him nearly every night in Lyttelton.' They had gone to Mrs Ward's where Ballinger 'rapped at the door'. When Mary Ward asked who was there he had replied, 'It's me,' and she had answered, 'You can't come in tonight, Harry.' Then the two men had walked away.

There was no mention of Mr Ward in all these proceedings, suggesting that Mary Ward was either a widow or separated. Or perhaps her husband had joined the rush to the West Coast goldfields. There must have been quite a few lonely women left to manage by themselves in Christchurch and Lyttelton after 1865. Wynn Williams had attempted to show that Ballinger and Mrs Ward were certainly not strangers, and Barker's testimony had clearly hinted at a relationship of some sort. Perhaps Ballinger's attentions had been welcomed for a while, but that day on the Bridle Path she had definitely said no. The jury retired for a long while, then returned with a verdict of not guilty.

Adultery and desertion were the subjects of a trial in the civil sittings of the Supreme Court in March 1867 that must have caused great scandal in the small community of German migrants living in

Canterbury. It was the old story of the eternal triangle, in which the friend of a married man made off with his younger wife. Wilhelmina Klaus had left her husband to live with his friend Grabau, and William Klaus was now seeking damages for their adultery so that he could obtain 'an act of divorcement' from the General Assembly, as the New Zealand parliament was then known. His problem was that he could not produce the marriage certificate, and the defence attempted to show that the couple had never been properly married. It was certainly an unusual household. The three of them lived for 11 months in a small one-room house in Lincoln Road. There were three beds, and Wilhelmina slept in a bed by herself. One friend said he had never seen William and Wilhelmina in bed together. Grabau had bought the house, and William had not lived there for more than a month before the trial.

Elizabeth Fuchs, wife of Joseph Fuchs, landlord of the Wellington Hotel, testified that the Klaus couple had stayed at the hotel, and had lived together as man and wife. Mr Klaus always called her Mrs Klaus. They had left and gone to Lyttelton in November 1866, but Mrs Klaus then returned to the hotel by herself in December, and stayed for two nights. On the third day Grabau came down and fetched her away with all her boxes:

> I saw Klaus about a fortnight afterwards. His wife afterwards came to the house to him, and they stayed together. After Klaus and his wife had gone to bed, Grabau came ... and asked where Mrs Klaus was. I told him that Mr and Mrs Klaus had gone to bed. Grabau said ... that he had a great mind to go up stairs and knock the old [bastard's] eye out. I told him not to forget that Klaus and his wife were married. Grabau said, 'Why does he not keep her?' I told him the number of the room in which they slept. He went up stairs, and I heard a great noise there. He came down greatly excited, and afterwards Mrs Klaus came down, and came into the bar after Grabau. She had some words with him; they used Low German language, which I did not understand. Grabau went and got a horse and cart ready, and

Mrs Klaus went and dressed herself and went away in the cart with him.

A baker named Christian Ditford, who had witnessed the row between Klaus and Grabau at the Wellington Hotel, told Grabau he should be ashamed of himself for taking away another man's wife. Grabau replied that he did not want her, and that she had come to him. Someone else had asked him how long he intended to keep her, and he replied, 'As long as I think proper.'

The prosecution called witnesses who had known the couple in London to testify that they had gone to the German church and heard the banns published before their wedding. The wife's maiden name had been Westball. Henry Muller had seen them coming from the church on what he supposed was their wedding day about five years before. Claus Burmeister said he remembered Mrs Klaus showing him her marriage certificate. Both witnesses knew all the parties involved. Muller had been a lodger in the Lincoln Road house with Klaus, Grabau and Wilhelmina, but did not say where they all slept. Klaus had sold some land to Grabau, and said that he and his wife were thinking of going to America.

Dr Foster for the defence contended that a marriage had not been proven, and that his client was entitled to a non-suit, but Mr Justice Gresson overruled this objection. Foster then argued that the damages, if any, should be very small, as the offence, if committed at all, had been committed after the charge had been laid. Henry Wynn Williams contended that the adultery had been fully proved, and that it was not strictly necessary to prove the marriage. If Mrs Klaus still had her marriage certificate, but wanted to live with Grabau, she was unlikely to produce it. Gresson reviewed all the relevant points of law, and spent some time in his summing-up, but the jury took only half an hour to agree on a verdict for the plaintiff on all counts. Damages were set at £40.

As with all of these cases, there is so much more that we would like to know. The evidence of friends and witnesses was only part of the full story. It would appear that Klaus was much older than

Wilhelmina, and perhaps had not provided for her as well as he had promised. The fact that she had run off with Grabau yet had gone back to Klaus suggests either a sense of duty or some lingering affection. There was no suggestion from any witness that Klaus had mistreated his wife. It sounds as if she was a confused and unhappy woman, torn between her marriage vows to an older man and her attraction to a younger man who was offering her a better future. Life is full of hard choices, and sometimes we live to regret the decisions that seemed the best ones at the time.

CHAPTER SIX

ARSON AND MURDER IN THE 1860S

Colombo Street, facing the Market Place, c. 1866. The shops in the middle of this photo are those that were destroyed in February 1868 in the suspected arson of the two-storey building owned by Rankin and Swales. Mrs Pope's shop was next door on the right. Swales was later executed for the murder of Rankin.

Canterbury Museum, CM 180

One case had all of Christchurch talking and speculating at the end of 1866: that of Darby Maher, who pleaded not guilty to charges of arson and murder. Maher owned two connected six-room cottages in lower Manchester Street, near the railway station, but had been sent to gaol for an unpaid debt, and while he was imprisoned his home and possessions had been sold by the mortgagee. When he was released early in November he had asked a law clerk, Edward Preston, what had become of his property, who had bought it and how much it had fetched. Preston told him it had been sold to George Allen and George Marshall at auction. Maher 'expressed himself much dissatisfied' at the price it had fetched, and said he should have been given notice of the sale. Next morning he called at his lawyer's office to ask how he could go about recovering his property. Preston saw him again later that day: 'He was then very drunk. He said he thought it was strange the property was sold whilst he was in gaol.' Maher repeated the same thing 'very strongly' to several other people, one recalling that he had said that if he could not get his house back he would burn it down.

Preston, who knew the place well, said it was rather dilapidated: the floorboards had 'shrunk very much, and altogether the house was shaky'. The new owners had put in a caretaker, an elderly man named Henry Smith. George Allen later told the court that Smith lived in the house, sleeping in an upstairs bedroom, and tended the garden. He was a 'sober steady man ... generally robust, and in good health'. Pender had never seen him the worse for drink. Smith had been pruning the overgrown hedge that surrounded the house, but had not cleared away all of the clippings. After Darby Maher had been released from gaol, Allen told Smith to be watchful, as he had heard strange rumours about him.

In the early hours of Sunday morning, 18 November 1866, a labourer named Henry Nachtigal was walking down Manchester Street towards the station when he saw smoke rising from the house previously owned by Darby Maher and flames through the windows. He ran to the Lichfield Street fire brigade station to raise the alarm, and then rushed back to the house: 'Through a back window I saw a man inside. He was in the back room on the floor. He looked black as if he were burnt. The doors were shut. I called out to him, but I think he was dead. I could not get near enough to break a window.'

When the fire bell in Lichfield Street began to ring, Inspector Pender, who was doing his rounds, saw the smoke and raced towards the fire. Among the neighbours gathering was George Allen, who said he was afraid Henry Smith was still in the house. When the fire started to subside, Pender went to the back of the house and saw what looked like a body.

By now quite a crowd had gathered, including Darby Maher. Several people, Pender among them, recognised him: 'I saw Maher there and from what I had heard previously, I had got a suspicion that he knew something about the fire. He was talking to Mr Collins. I heard him say, "It would be all right except [for] that," pointing to the dead body. He was very uneasy.'

Constable Feast now joined Pender and told him that he had seen Maher about 12.20am near the corner of George and Manchester streets, coming out from under the hedge near where the fire later broke out. Feast had followed Maher into town, and saw him in front of the City Hotel in High Street, but then lost him. Feast patrolled Cathedral Square for a while, then heard the fire bell and ran back down Manchester Street. He was surprised to see Darby Maher already there, talking to Collins. When Feast asked him, 'Have you not seen the property since you came out of gaol?' Maher replied, 'I have never been lower than the White Hart.' (This hotel was on High Street between Hereford and Lichfield streets.) But Feast knew he was lying, so he reported the conversation to Inspector Pender and they arrested Maher on suspicion of arson and murder.

The inquest into the death of Henry Smith began the next day, 19 November, and took two days, as there were so many witnesses to be heard. William Collins said that he had been talking to Mr Tombs at the corner of Barbadoes and Cashel streets about 1am on Sunday when they saw a fire across the fields. They ran as far as the Provincial Hotel in lower Barbadoes Street and were going to raise the alarm when the fire bell rang out. Going down Manchester Street they caught up with Darby Maher. Collins spoke to him, and Maher said, 'Do you know my name?' They went on a little further and Maher said it was his house on fire. Collins asked if anyone was living in it, and Maher replied that someone was 'bachelorising there, or something to that effect'. Maher said he had not been near the place for three months. Collins thought Maher had been drinking.

John Newson testified that he had seen Darby Maher walking up and down in front of the City Hotel just before midnight: 'He appeared tipsy at the time.' A blacksmith named John Mannington, a resident of George Street and one of the first on the scene, saw a man inside the hedge whom he now knew to be Darby Maher. He was standing looking at the fire. There could not have been more than one or two other onlookers. Maher was making no attempt to put out the fire, which was coming through the roof on the south side. The fire bell had not then been rung.

The inquest jury, satisfied that the circumstantial evidence linked Maher to the scene of the crime, returned a verdict of death by wilful murder. Maher was committed for trial in the Supreme Court.

The trial opened on 6 December before Mr Justice Gresson. Much of the evidence already heard at the inquest was repeated for the benefit of the jury, and occupied most of the first day. The jury was 'locked up for the night' and the trial resumed on 7 December. Maher pleaded not guilty, and the defence produced several witnesses who said he was 'a quite inoffensive man', somewhat addicted to drinking, but otherwise harmless. In May 1863 he had sold most of his town section on Manchester Street, except the half-acre on which the house stood, for about £2000. But his investments then went wrong and he had lost it all and gone deeply into debt, finishing up in prison. Auctioneer Joseph Bennett said Maher was a very honest and harmless man, occasionally addicted to drinking.

The prosecution brought several more witnesses to testify that Maher had been 'very much the worse for drink' that night, and had been refused a bed where he had been staying, at Uncle Tom's Coffee House in the Triangle, near the City Hotel, because he was drunk.

Maher's defence lawyer, Henry Wynn Williams, addressed the jury at length. He first raised the possibility that the deceased may have contributed to his own death by going back into the house after the fire had started. But the jurors would have remembered Inspector Pender's testimony that the front door was nailed shut and the bolt on the back door had not been withdrawn. A man entering a burning house would surely not bolt the door behind him. Wynn Williams said that the testimony of several of the witnesses could be disregarded. Constable Feast had said he had found a lot of matches in Maher's pocket, but he did not say that he also found a pipe.

The jury should consider carefully before they consigned a man to 'ignominious death by hanging': the evidence was all circumstantial, and if they had any doubts they must acquit.

Crown prosecutor Thomas Duncan admitted that the evidence was circumstantial, but said there were reliable witnesses who linked Maher to the crime scene before and after the fire. Duncan placed great weight on Allen's testimony that Maher had said that if the property was taken from him he would burn it. Acting under the influence of alcohol, he had done just that. It was also apparent that he knew the elderly caretaker slept in the house. In starting the fire he had shown a callous disregard for human life.

In his summing-up, Gresson agreed that the evidence was all presumptive and circumstantial. He noted that malice was essential to the crime of murder, but in law malice need not necessarily be expressed. It could also be implied: 'If a man acted in so reckless a manner as would probably cause the death of a human being he would be held responsible for the consequences.' If the jury believed that Maher had deliberately set fire to the house, 'it would not matter whether he knew Smith was in it at the time. If Smith was in the house and lost his life from the fire, they must find the prisoner guilty of murder, although there was no proof of malice.'

The jury retired at 5.30pm, and returned 20 minutes later with a verdict of not guilty. Maher was then arraigned on the charge of arson, but Duncan said he did not intend to proceed with this indictment, and the jury, by Gresson's direction, returned a verdict of not guilty. Gresson then addressed Maher and told him that he had been brought into his present position by his unfortunate habit of drinking, and he hoped that he would abstain from it in future. The prisoner was then discharged.

In the early hours of 5 November 1867 the headmaster's house at Christ's College was burned to the ground. Arson was suspected from the start, yet there were no obvious suspects, apart from the boarders, some of whom may have resented the strict discipline of the new headmaster, the Reverend William Chambers Harris. Though he was a young man, a graduate of Brasenose College, Oxford, his magnificent bushy beard made him appear much older. He was a vigorous, athletic, efficient headmaster who believed in caning as the best way to tame the 'young savages' entrusted to his charge. His wife and young son, 13 boys and two servants lived with him in the rambling wooden headmaster's house, which had dormer bedrooms, five brick chimneys and a bell-tower.

The blaze, which started in the gutter between two gables at the rear end of the house, was first noticed by a servant, Marion Reese, who woke her colleague in the next bedroom, then ran to wake the headmaster. He roused the boys, sent one to alert the fire brigade and organised the rest into a bucket chain from the nearby Avon River. As other people arrived he set them to work removing furniture and books from the house and schoolroom. Though all the fire bells were being rung soon after 2am, the firemen had great trouble starting the steam engine *Extinguisher*, and there was much confusion about the exact location of the fire. The manual pump *Dreadnought* was not on the scene until 3.20am, after rushing up Papanui Road (or Whately Road as it then was) in the wrong direction. By this time the house had been completely destroyed, and the firemen could only dampen the embers and make sure no sparks were smouldering on nearby buildings.

The inquest into the fire held on 14 November found no obvious cause, and no obvious suspects. There had been four or five other serious fires early in that dry summer, and many people were convinced that a 'fire-bug' was at work. The police made no further progress in their enquiries until 1870, when Sergeant Thomas O'Grady had an interesting conversation with a man in the Lion Hotel at Rangiora in North Canterbury. As a result of his report, Inspector Pender arrested Walter ('Watty') Neillas on 28 May 1870 and charged him with the arson of the headmaster's house at Christ's College in 1867. The Canterbury *Police Gazette* described him as an older man, aged 60, 5ft 8in (172cm) tall – a good height in those days – with a fresh complexion, grey hair and brown eyes, a flat nose and 'very coarse features'.

Appearing before Mr Justice Gresson in the Supreme Court on 16 June 1870, Neillas pleaded not guilty. The Reverend Harris, Marion Reese and Inspector Pender all gave evidence. Sergeant O'Grady recounted his conversation with Neillas in Rangiora, which had started in the bar but then moved to a bedroom. According to O'Grady, Neillas wanted to make a confession about the 1867 fire, saying he 'saw the whole thing done', but got diverted and agitated about Police Sergeant-Major Pardy, his rival at that time for the affections of one Amelia Levy, swearing to kill him if he had the chance. He broke off, saying he would tell O'Grady more in the morning, but he never did. Three weeks later O'Grady met Neillas in the street and said, 'Well, Watty, you haven't come to tell me that yet.' Neillas had replied, 'No, I have not, but I will before I go, as I will do you a good turn.' Gresson rebuked the sergeant for going 'to the very verge of his duty', adding that '[t]he police should not be instrumental in any way in wresting information'.

Amelia Levy, who was the key witness for the prosecution, said she was then living at the corner of Durham and Peterborough streets, where Neillas was a frequent visitor, 'backwards and forwards at my house', but was not living with her. He was at her house on the evening of the fire, between 5 and 6pm. Then he came back and knocked at her door just before dawn, and said that the college was on fire: had she not heard the bell? When she said no, he said, 'You'll hear it soon.' He told her he had been at the fire but had run away from it. When she remarked that this behaviour would lead to his being suspected of arson, he replied that they might suspect him if they liked: '[I]t was a beautiful sight, and he hoped it would be burnt to the ground; it would be a little work for the plasterers.' He then told her he had helped to burn a house down once before, but would not say where or when: 'He said he wanted work, and would like to see a few more places burnt down.'

Amelia Levy went on to say that Neillas had once asked her for canvas to make tea and sugar bags. He wanted 'sufficient canvas for a square bag'. When she gave him 'nearly a square yard of canvas', she commented that 'it was a strange thing to put tea and sugar in'. Under cross-examination by defence counsel Henry Wynn Williams she admitted that she had come out to New Zealand two and a half years earlier 'under the name of Calvert', though on board the ship she had been called Maggie O'Connor since she did not wish her name to be 'known as an immigrant'. Immediately after arriving in Christchurch she had changed her name to Amelia Levy: 'I forget now with whom I lived after coming here ... I stayed at Mrs Green's some time. [Neillas] never supplied me with money, clothing, or food. He never acted as a friend, nor did he ever live with me.'

At this point Gresson intervened and told the witness she did not have to answer these questions. Wynn Williams urged the judge to compel her to answer, as he was testing her credibility. Gresson retorted that the questioning was 'degrading and irrelevant', and declined to order her to answer. Under further questioning Amelia Levy admitted that she had once prosecuted Neillas for assault, but denied the suggestion that there had been any familiarity between herself and Sergeant-Major Pardy. She denied ever wearing a locket with Pardy's likeness in it: 'No man lived with me since I came to New Zealand.' But she then admitted that she had had two children since her arrival. Wynn Williams asked incredulously, 'And did no man ever visit you?'

Inspector Pender concluded the evidence for the prosecution by recalling that there had been three or four attempted arsons within six weeks of the college fire – at St Luke's schoolhouse, at St Michael's schoolhouse and at the Devonshire Arms, near where the prisoner lived. All had started in the roof gutter between gables: 'I found in a gutter at the Devonshire Arms some gorse and other material sewed up in canvas. The piece of canvas and gorse had been slightly on fire. It was made up in a little square bag about 12 inches long by 9 or 10 broad ... I didn't find any other bag elsewhere.' The bag had presumably been lit, then tossed up onto the roof to set fire to the wooden shingles, but the flame had gone out.

In his address to the jury Wynn Williams stressed that though suspicious circumstances had been described, the Crown had failed to prove the prisoner's guilt, and there was not sufficient evidence to warrant a conviction. He entirely discredited Amelia Levy's evidence as that of an unreliable witness, and asked the jury for an acquittal. The jury agreed with him, returning after a short while with a verdict of not guilty.

If, however, Amelia Levy was telling the truth and not making up a story out of spite, it seems just possible that Walter Neillas was indeed the Christchurch fire-bug of 1867. He could not be convicted on hearsay evidence, and a jury of respectable citizens was unlikely to take any notice of the testimony of a woman who admitted to having two illegitimate children, while denying that she had ever lived with Neillas or any other man. As Don Hamilton remarks in his excellent history of Christ's College, two virgin births were a bit much for a Christchurch jury to swallow. The suspected arsonist walked free.

In the 1860s the Market Place was a much livelier place than Cathedral Square, as it was surrounded by stables and pubs and shops, with Cobb & Co. coaches heading out over the Victoria Bridge and the mail service to Lyttelton coming and going each day.

Early in February 1868 it was the scene of no fewer than three classic calamities: flood, fire and murder. The flood came first, on 4 February, when the Waimakariri River burst its banks and overflowed into the headwaters of the Avon. The little river rose alarmingly during the morning, even though the weather was fine and warm. By evening the Market Place was entirely under water, and the Worcester Street footbridge had been swept away. Many homes had been flooded, and the old Land Office on Worcester Street had been inundated by 3ft (almost a metre) of water. City council records and the papers of the Magistrate's Court had been removed to the Police Barracks in the Market Place and stowed safely upstairs. After the flood peaked at midnight the water level quickly returned to normal, and daybreak revealed a dismal scene of mud and debris.

Only a few days after the flood, the fire brigade had to deal with a major fire almost on its own doorstep. John Rankin and John Densley Swales ran a grocery store on Colombo Street, opposite the post office. The fire station was a stone's throw beyond the post office, on the Armagh Street side of the Market Place. Rankin and Swales lived on the premises, in an upstairs bedroom. Rankin was the older of the two; Swales was 56. Though they were business partners they were not friends. Neighbours often heard them arguing, and sometimes shouting at each other. These disagreements appeared to be either about money – the business was not thriving – or Swales's excessive drinking. Rankin had also objected that 'certain women' kept coming to the back door asking for Swales: 'they were not decent'. John Cass, a butcher who knew both men well, said they 'very often growled at each other'. He had frequently heard Swales complain that Rankin was a lazy old man, 'sleepy and pig-headed'.

The day before the fire Isaac Allen, another neighbour who knew both men, had heard Swales offer to buy Rankin's share of the business, and Swales had asked Allen if he would consider a business partnership with him. Mrs Elizabeth Smith, wife of the proprietor of the Duke of Wellington Hotel on Colombo Street, had heard Swales say on the afternoon before the fire that 'business was very dull' and he was thinking of going to Melbourne. Her husband had heard Swales remark in his bar on the night of the fire, 'All we want is a fire after the flood to ruin us utterly.'

Next door to Swales and Rankin's store, Mrs Sarah Ann Pope lived at the back of her fancygoods shop. It was in a room in her quarters that she spent the evening of 7 February sewing at a table. The walls of the two wooden buildings were only a few inches apart. About 10pm she heard a noise like the locking of a door, as if Rankin and Swales were shutting up their shop. She heard nothing more until, just after 11pm, there were several crashes as of shelves and bottles falling, and a sound 'like the crackling of a fire'. When she pulled aside the window blind she saw that Swales and Rankin's house was on fire, with flames coming through the roof of the lean-to.

> Swale[s] was standing at the bottom of the garden, inside the
> fence, looking at the flames. He was dressed in dark clothes, and
> had on what is generally called a belltopper. He looked completely
> dressed, just the same as he would be on a Sunday ... He was
> standing quietly looking at the fire. He was not giving any alarm
> of fire, as if he had been I must have heard it ... He remained
> standing in the garden as long as I stood at the window.

Mrs Pope immediately ran out into the street and from the front of
the burning building 'looked through their shop windows and saw
that all was dark'. When she glanced up at the roof she could see
'smoke coming over as if from the back'.

When Mrs Pope shouted 'Fire!' several people appeared from
the nearby hotels, including Rebecca Money, wife of the proprietor of the Victoria Hotel. She then went to warn the people at
the Market Hotel. Her husband, Charles, had also seen the flames
coming through the roof of Rankin's lean-to. He had rushed back
into the hotel to rouse their boarders and lodgers, and saw them
all safely out of the front door into Colombo Street. There he saw
Swales standing in front of the post office, fully dressed and wearing
a top hat. Mrs Pope also saw Swales standing quietly there. Men were
knocking at the door of Rankin's store, but it was locked. Mrs Money
said, 'What a dreadful thing, Mr Swales, your house is on fire!' and he
calmly replied, 'Yes, Mrs Money, my house is on fire.' She then asked
if the old man had got out and he said he did not know; he had had
enough to do to get himself out.

The fire brigade had trundled their old hand-pump across from
the station, but its feeble stream had little effect as the fire quickly
engulfed the whole of the store. Horses were fetched from the stables
on Armagh Street and harnessed to *Extinguisher*, while the engineer
raised steam and a suction hose was run down to the Avon River. But
the horses took fright at the large crowd now assembled, and there
was some delay before 'copious streams of water' could be played
on the flames. Several men helped to remove stock from Mrs Pope's
shop, which had now caught alight, and Captain Wilson of the fire

brigade ordered his men to pull down an empty shop between Mrs Pope's and the Market Hotel to create a fire break. On the northern side of Swales and Rankin's store a shoe shop and an empty cottage at the back were now 'burning furiously'.

During the fire a rumour spread among the crowd that a man had been inside the store when the fire started, and he had not come out. Isaac Allen recognised Swales standing in front of the post office, and Swales said to him, 'Poor Rankin has not got out of the fire. I'm afraid he's burnt.' He told Inspector Pender that he had been woken by the smell of smoke, and had called to Rankin, who 'gave a snore and turned over in the bed, but did not move'. Swales said he had grabbed his clothes and run downstairs through the flames into the yard. Pender, somewhat excitedly, said, 'You're a damned curious fellow that you're not looking for your mate!' Others listening made similar remarks.

As soon as the flames had been doused the police and firemen began to search the ruins. Captain Wilson called to Pender and pointed to a blackened body lying where the front door had been. Pender sent for Dr Marshall and dispatched a constable to find Swales. On seeing the body Swales said, 'That must be Rankin. He must have fallen down from where he was sleeping, bed and all.' There were pieces of charred mattress and parts of a bed frame under the body. Pender had difficulty in getting Swales to stop and look at the clothes: '[H]e drew away two or three times.' The inspector then 'set a constable to watch him'. Isaac Allen identified the trousers as the ones Rankin had been wearing that day. The body was removed to the fire station 'in Dr Marshall's presence', and then to the hospital, where it was locked in the morgue.

About 3am Swales turned up at the Victoria Hotel, where a group of men and women were drinking and talking about the fire. When Charles Money asked Swales if he knew how the fire had started, he replied that there was some kerosene in the lean-to and he thought it had started there. He then repeated his story about trying to rouse Rankin, and running downstairs through the flames. One side of his face and whiskers had been scorched but his clothes were unmarked.

Money, curious, asked Swales if he was dressed when the fire broke out. Swales said no, he was undressed: he had carried his clothes over his arm through the flames, then got dressed in the yard. Money looked at his collar and neat necktie; Swales said he had worn them to bed. Money then looked at his boots, which were laced up; Swales said he had tied them in the yard. Money then asked if he had lost everything in the fire, but Swales said he had tossed his carpet-bag into the yard, where he expected the police would soon find it.

Among the men at the bar was Rankin's landlord, one Mr Walton, who had been drinking a few too many (Pender later said he was drunk). Walton asked Swales, 'Didn't you tell me that either you or your partner had set the place on fire?' but Swales refused to answer such a question in a public bar. Walton cursed and said: 'You're a bloody old rogue!'

Swales then turned up at the Duke of Wellington, where Elizabeth Smith recalled his arrival about 4.30am. He asked her for a bed but they had no rooms available. She asked him where Rankin was but he made no reply. She then mentioned the fire, and he said, 'What fire?' When she replied, 'The fire in your house', he said he had no idea of any such event. He then asked for a 'nobbler' (a glass of spirits) but she refused, thinking he had already had too much to drink.

Swales went back to the Victoria Hotel, where Inspector Pender and Detective Feast found him about 5am. As people questioned Swales about the fire he repeated his story about running out through the flames, but when they asked about Rankin he said, 'You want to know too much.' Pender requested him to step outside and then told him he was under arrest on suspicion of arson and murder, and cautioned him. Swales replied, 'My Lord, you don't mean that,' and said he was sorry for the old man. He then walked off, saying they had no right to arrest him, but Pender and Feast reasoned with him and he finally stopped and said he would go quietly. (One newspaper more dramatically said that he had to be dragged to the police station.)

About 9am on the morning of 8 February Charles Money searched the yard behind the Victoria Hotel and discovered a carpet-bag leaning against an empty barrel, next to the fence. It was on the side nearest Rankin's store. He handed it straight to a police constable, who took it to Inspector Pender. When opened it was found to contain neatly folded clothes and an account book, inside which was an insurance policy for £400 covering the furniture, fittings and stock-in-trade of the grocery store.

This narrative has been reconstructed from a large body of detailed testimony given at the inquest held on 10 February and at the Supreme Court trial, which opened before Mr Justice Gresson on 5 March 1868. Thomas Duncan was the Crown prosecutor, and Henry Wynn Williams defended. Swales was indicted on two counts: the wilful murder of Rankin, and arson causing the death of a person unknown – just in case the jury had any doubts about the identification of the body. He pleaded not guilty. The trial, which occupied three days, aroused intense public interest. In his final address to the jury Duncan pointed out the many inconsistencies in Swales's various statements to his neighbours, and stressed that he had both motive and opportunity to commit the crime. He may have killed Rankin in his bed, or rendered him unconscious, relying on the fire to destroy all the evidence. The carefully packed bag and the insurance policy seemed to confirm his intention to depart, as he had told various people, for Melbourne.

Wynn Williams called no witnesses but spoke at length, pointing out that the evidence against Swales was all circumstantial and presumptive. He suggested that the fire had started in the empty shop next door, then spread to the lean-to and its store of kerosene. Swales had woken, grabbed his bag and clothes, attempted to rouse Rankin, then run downstairs through the flames, getting his face scorched on the way. Rankin was overcome by the smoke and perished in the fire. Swales may have been foolish, or befuddled by the drink he had consumed that evening, but Williams asserted he would have to have been a lunatic to behave as he did after the event if indeed he was guilty of the crime. He had stayed at the scene and talked to his neighbours, whereas a guilty person would have disappeared quickly. His story had inconsistencies, but these could also be attributed to his drinking. He had denied the crime when Pender arrested him, and had gone quietly to the lockup. He still denied the murder charge.

The jury retired for only 20 minutes and returned with a guilty verdict, but added a recommendation for mercy, as the evidence was circumstantial. Mr Justice Gresson replied, 'I do not understand you. Such a recommendation implies a doubt on your part as to the guilt of the prisoner. If such is the case you had better reconsider your verdict.' The jurymen talked among themselves without leaving the jury box, and their foreman finally said they were all agreed on a guilty verdict. When Gresson asked Swales if he had anything to say he shook his head and said no. Gresson then said he agreed with the verdict and that it was now his duty, painful though it might be, to pass a sentence of death. After donning the black cap he sentenced Swales to death by hanging. He advised the condemned man to make the best use of his remaining time to make his peace with God, and that he should not entertain any hope of a remission or commutation of his sentence. Swales showed no emotion.

While awaiting his execution Swales told police that he had often thought of setting fire to the shop for the insurance money but he had never intended to kill Rankin. He wrote two lengthy statements, in one of which he resigned his 'most precious and immortal soul into the hands of my blessed saviour'. On the day of his execution, 16 April 1868, two clergymen visited Swales at 6am and prayed with him. He was reported to be calm and taciturn. The police had kept the date of his execution secret in order to prevent any curious onlookers from gathering on the hillside above the prison. John Densley Swales died on the scaffold at 8.15am, the first man to be executed at the Lyttelton Gaol.

Mrs Pope's shop had been insured for £1500 but she had lost about £500 worth of stock in the fire and from water damage. Walton, the owner of the building leased by Rankin and Swales, had been away in Australia and had returned only a week or two before the fire to discover that his agent had forgotten to renew his insurance policy. He suffered a total loss, as did the owner of the two smaller unoccupied buildings, also uninsured.

The inquest on Rankin's death, the police charge sheet and the Supreme Court proceedings all gave the prisoner's name as John Densley Swale, but his real name was Swales. Oddly enough, another family with the name Swale had a shop in the Market Place for many years but were not related to the arsonist-murderer of 1868. Mrs Pope opened a new shop a few doors along in Colombo Street and traded there until 1893. Her business survived in other hands, but retaining her name, until the late twentieth century, as one of Christchurch's best-known retailers of fabrics, ribbons and sewing supplies.

Although historians have no means of reconstructing the mental processes whereby a jury reaches its verdict, as jurors are bound to keep silent about their deliberations, the newspapers often gave their names, and occasionally we can discover what sorts of people were empanelled. For example, in the fierce debates over the temperance movement in the 1890s one licensing jury happened to be composed almost entirely of prohibitionists, who shut down all the pubs in Sydenham for a short time. But it is much harder to unpick the composition of 1860s juries, when the public records are scantier. No well-known names stand out in the jury lists for these two arson and murder trials.

What the juries saw and heard, now lost to us, were the demeanour and tone of voice of the witnesses and the accused. This is why appeal courts are still so reluctant to overturn a jury verdict. A sullen and silent prisoner, as Swales appears to have been, would not win much sympathy when the circumstantial evidence against him seemed so persuasive. Yet even when the evidence seemed highly persuasive, as in the Darby Maher case, some juries refused to convict, probably heeding the usual defence plea that if they had even the slightest doubt they should acquit, rather than send an innocent person to their death. The jury's recommendation for mercy in the case of Swales suggests that some of the jurors at least had doubts about his guilt, but fell into line when the judge insisted that they make up their minds.

On the basis of the written record of evidence presented in the two high-profile cases of Darby Maher and John Swales it seems possible that one or both of the juries got it wrong. Maher's 'not guilty' verdict was a surprise to everyone, not least himself, whereas most of his neighbours seem to have assumed that Swales was guilty of murder in an insurance fraud arson. Arson was a common crime in nineteenth-century Christchurch, yet the culprits were rarely caught. The fire brigade was often called out to hedge fires in the night, especially in the dry summer months, and empty wooden shops were an obvious target for vagrants and vandals. Had the crashing of shelves and bottles heard by Mrs Pope been caused by a burglar whose candle set fire to the kerosene in the lean-to?

If Swales had wanted to burn down the shop for the insurance, and Rankin with it, why did he set the fire in the early evening when so many people were still up and about? It would have been smarter to start the fire in the dead of the night, and to give himself an alibi by sleeping elsewhere, perhaps in the house on the East Belt (later Fitzgerald Avenue) that we know he had rented from John Lewis on the morning of 7 February. We may never know. Swales could have been an alcoholic and a depressive who simply resigned himself to his fate when he saw the cards so comprehensively stacked against him. But he may also have been a murderer.

CHAPTER SEVEN

THE MONAGHAN CASE: MURDER OR MANSLAUGHTER?

THE SENSATIONAL.
News-vendor – 'Now, my man, what is it?'
Boy – 'I vonts a nillustrated newspaper with a norrid murder and a likeness in it.'

John Leech, *Four Hundred Humorous Illustrations*, 2nd edn, 1862

I n Oxford Terrace, across the river from the Antigua Boatsheds, there still stands one of the oldest surviving wooden houses in Christchurch, albeit on new foundations. It is now known as the Pegasus Arms, having been the premises of the Pegasus Press for several decades after the Second World War. The front part was originally built in 1852 as a property speculation for the merchants Longdon and Le Cren. They soon sold it to the first surgeon-general of Christchurch Hospital, and the next three owners were all medical men. The first meeting of the Canterbury Medical Association was held here in 1865. By 1868 the house was occupied by Dr John W. S. Coward, a general practitioner who was also the district coroner.

Early in the morning of 7 March 1868 Dr Coward was roused from his bed by a policeman who asked him to come quickly as a man had been stabbed:

> I proceeded to the junction of the Lincoln and Riccarton Roads. I saw there a person on the ground, surrounded by several who were assisting him. Hearing that he had been stabbed in the chest, I advised them to take the man to the hospital. I accompanied him there, and delivered him into the charge of Dr Powell, the house surgeon.

Dr Llewellyn Powell now takes up the story:

> On the morning of 7th March last a man was brought to the hospital ... His name was given as George Frisby. He was in a state of collapse. There was a punctured wound on the left side of his chest, between the second and third ribs and within an inch of the breast bone. I did not probe it. I sat with him until he somewhat recovered. He showed symptoms of pleurisy ...

Powell placed lint on the wound to keep out the air but 'the side of the chest became enlarged from the collection of fluid, and on the morning of the 14th March the fluid burst through the wound. From that time he gradually sank; the right lung became inflamed and he died on the morning of the 1st April.' Powell considered that Frisby 'was originally a very healthy man'.

> I made a post-mortem examination of the body. I found a wound penetrating into the left cavity of the chest, between second and third ribs. There was pus in the chest. The lung itself was compressed and bound down to the back of the chest from inflammation ... The right lung was in a state of advanced inflammation. The other organs were all healthy. In my opinion death was caused by the suppuration of the pleura, and inflammation of the right lung, caused by exhaustion and blood poisoning, and these were caused by the stab wound. The marks in the clothes would correspond with the wound. Frisby died in the hospital. I do not believe he ever left it ...

The constable who had summoned Dr Coward, Patrick Grace, stayed with the men who had been helping Frisby. They told him he had been stabbed by a man called Monaghan outside the house of their friend, Mrs Heyward. Grace followed them along Lincoln Road (now part of Hagley Avenue) to the house occupied by Sarah Heyward and her children. There he concealed himself until he heard a noise and saw a man near the wall. On being challenged, the man identified himself as William Henry Monaghan, and Constable Grace arrested him on a charge of stabbing George Frisby. While being cautioned, Monaghan took out a pocket-knife and gave it to the constable, saying that this was the weapon he had used to stab the man. Though the knife had some blood and rust on it, there was no blood on Monaghan's clothing.

After the inquest on Frisby, which returned a verdict of death by murder or manslaughter, and the hearing in the Magistrate's Court that committed him for trial in the Supreme Court, Monaghan remained in custody at the Lyttelton Gaol. He had given his age as 25 years. The Supreme Court trial opened on 3 June 1868.

The Crown prosecutor was Thomas Duncan, as usual, but the defence was conducted by Dr Charles James Foster, whom we met in Chapter 5, one of the most brilliant academic lawyers in nineteenth-century Christchurch. He was a graduate of University College, London, where he had been appointed a law fellow and professor of jurisprudence. Active in politics and university reform, he wrote a textbook on jurisprudence before coming out to New Zealand in 1864. He was appointed city solicitor in 1866, but found it hard to make a living on the few cases that matched his expertise, and was declared bankrupt in 1869. When Canterbury (University) College was founded in 1873 he was appointed lecturer in law, and then in jurisprudence, but the depression of the 1880s meant that few students came his way.

The first witness for the prosecution was miner John Richard Gibbs, who was living at the Glasgow Arms in Antigua Street with his mate George Frisby early in 1868. On the evening in question, while the two men were having a beer after supper, Sarah Heyward came into the hotel. After about half an hour in her company they left with her to see her home. On the way they were joined by a young man named William Kerr. All four called in at the White Horse, before they

proceeded to a house behind the Rev Mr Fraser's, situated off the Lincoln Road. Frisby and Mrs Heyward went into the house, and I followed at her request. We passed through the front room into a second. There was a man there in bed [Monaghan]. He had come to the door to let us in and had gone back to bed. He appeared to be angry with Mrs Heyward, and she told him not to be so, as she knew the friends of Frisby and myself at home [England], and wanted us to see her two boys, as we were going home.

After some further conversation, which Gibbs could not recall, Frisby had said to Monaghan, 'Here, mate, don't be cross, have a drink.' Monaghan agreed and took the drink, 'which was gin – whether Old Tom or Hollands I don't know'. They were in the house about half an hour altogether and Monaghan seemed a little more sociable than he had been at first.

I said, 'We'll go home now, George.' He said, 'I have some apples and nuts. I will give them to the children.' I heard him speak to the children, who were in bed in the front room, as I left the door to go out. I joined William Kerr in the open air, leaving Frisby inside the house. Before I had gone five yards, Frisby came to it. Kerr was 20 or 30 yards from the door ... I went back to the front door to ask Frisby to come home. The woman (Mrs Heyward) kept us talking for some time ... The prisoner came to the door in his shirt, and told Mrs Heyward to come inside. She said, 'All right, Bill, I'll be in in a few minutes.' Mrs Heyward began crying and said, 'Oh, what would my friends say if they saw me like this?'

Monaghan, who had gone back into the house, soon returned and said to Sarah Heyward, 'Now, do you mean to come into the house? If you don't, I'll do something for you.' When he threatened to strike her, Gibbs said, 'Mate, you won't strike her while I'm present.' Monaghan responded, 'Won't I? I'll let you see; I'll put this (holding up a knife) into the first bloody man who interferes with me.' He ordered the weeping woman into the house two or three times. When he made a move towards her she shrank behind Gibbs, saying, 'Oh, Bill, don't strike me!' 'Don't be angry, mate,' said Frisby, stepping between Gibbs and Monaghan.

> Monaghan made a blow or kind of push at Frisby, and knocked his hat off. Frisby then struck him on the cheek, I believe, but cannot be positive, with his open hand – first with his left, then with his right immediately after. The second blow struck Monaghan on the left cheekbone; they were not severe blows as they did not make the slightest mark ... Monaghan immediately struck Frisby with the knife and ran away.

Gibbs and Kerr went up to Frisby and asked him, 'What's the matter, George?' He replied, 'I am stabbed.' They took off his coat and shirt and saw the wound on his chest: 'It was bleeding pretty freely.' They tied a handkerchief around his chest to try to stop the bleeding, but he complained of feeling very weak and fell down. Two men came up, and were sent off to fetch a doctor and the police. Gibbs and Kerr supported Frisby until Dr Coward came, then helped to get him across the road to the hospital.

Under cross-examination by Dr Foster, Gibbs added some further details. He had not met Sarah Heyward before that night, but Frisby had known her in England. They had all had several drinks in the course of the evening. There was a candle burning in the front bedroom, and Gibbs said he saw the blade of the knife twice, quite distinctly. Monaghan had no knife in his hand when he first came to the door to ask the woman to come inside: 'The scuffle was all over in a moment; I was simply standing; it was so sudden that I could do nothing; Mrs Heyward, who came behind my back for protection from her husband, was holding my arm at the time the prisoner struck the blow [at Frisby] with the knife.'

William Kerr, a labourer, confirmed Gibbs's evidence. Then Sarah Heyward took the witness stand and told the court that she was the wife of William Heyward, a labourer, but they had separated, and Monaghan had been living with her and keeping her for nine months before March. Monaghan had got out of bed to speak to Frisby and Gibbs, as they were friends of hers and soon leaving for Britain on the *Melita*, and she wanted them to see her boys:

> Monaghan said to me he was surprised at my being out so late. He drank with them. Frisby told him he was going home in the *Melita*, and had come to see me and the boys. I then said to Monaghan, 'I am going to speak to Frisby.' Monaghan said, 'I don't want you out so late at night.' I said, 'Frisby, or Gibbs, if you are going home, see my father and tell him how I am situated.' This happened at the step of the front door. It was while I was standing there that Monaghan called me in, and I went to bed. Monaghan went out of the house with nothing on but his shirt. He was not in the house when I went to bed. On my oath, I do not know where he had gone.

At this point Mr Justice Gresson interrupted and observed that her version of events was different from that of Gibbs and Kerr. He warned her that she 'seemed to be trifling with the truth' and he would consider whether she should be committed for perjury.

Sarah Heyward admitted that she could not remember whether Monaghan had come out in his shirt while she was talking to Frisby and Gibbs; he might have done so. She had seen the knife on the table before she went out that night. She told Monaghan that she would not be away more than an hour or an hour and a half. While she was drinking with Frisby and Gibbs they had both made 'improper proposals', and Frisby had repeated them just outside the door of her house:

> Monaghan must have heard it or I don't think he would have been so excited. Frisby and Gibbs were about half-an-hour in the house ... I swear that I left Monaghan, Gibbs, and Frisby in

> the kitchen when I went to bed; I am quite certain of that. They
> appeared to be on friendly terms. I heard a scream as though it
> came from the bottom of the right-of-way about ten minutes
> afterwards ... I swear I didn't hear Frisby or Gibbs say a word
> when Monaghan threatened me ... I never saw Frisby or Gibbs
> interfering to prevent Monaghan from striking me, to the best of
> my recollection.

Once again Mr Justice Gresson interrupted and reminded her that
the words 'to the best of my recollection' would not save her from
a charge of perjury.

Mrs Heyward's cross-examination did not improve. She could
not remember the sequence of events or give a coherent account of
herself. She admitted that she had not said anything about Frisby
or Gibbs wanting to take 'improper liberties' with her when she
gave evidence in the Magistrate's Court. She had told Dr Foster a
fortnight ago. She denied taking any drink into the bedroom but
the Crown prosecutor read from her depositions in which she had
stated that she went into the bedroom where Monaghan was, and
Frisby had followed, and they drank together. Gresson said he would
consider whether to grant Mr Duncan's request to commit Sarah
Heyward for perjury.

The next witness was her elder son, William Charles Heyward,
a lad of 14, who gave his testimony in a clear and straightforward
manner:

> I was in bed when my mother and the two men came home.
> Monaghan was in bed. My mother came into the house first,
> Frisby next, and then Gibbs. They went into the kitchen, and
> then into the bedroom where Monaghan was. They began
> chatting with each other, and Frisby wanted Monaghan to drink.
> Monaghan drank about 10 minutes after being asked. I think
> they were in the bedroom with Monaghan about a quarter of
> an hour. Gibbs went out of the house first, Frisby followed,
> and my mother after. My brother went out, and I followed. My
> mother went a little of the road with Frisby and Gibbs, and then

Monaghan came out and told her to come in. She said, 'All right', and turned back, and so did Frisby and Gibbs. Monaghan had returned to bed.

It was when Sarah Heyward, Frisby and Gibbs were chatting outside the house, a few yards from the door, that Monaghan reappeared and said, 'Come in, Sarah, else I'll strike you'. He went back to bed, 'and my mother followed him'. Frisby and Gibbs went away but returned, entered the house and gave young William and his brother a pear and some nuts. 'They went away, came back, and went out again – Frisby, Monaghan, and Gibbs together, and began quarrelling. He had the knife in his hand; he had just finished cutting up some tobacco.'

The boy saw Frisby striking Monaghan 'with his fist somewhere on the arm'. Monaghan then told him to leave, 'saying it was quite time for any man to be at home'. After Frisby struck Monaghan a second time, Monaghan said, 'If you strike me again I will put this knife into you.' Frisby hit him again, this time on the back, and Monaghan 'went at him' and 'put the knife in him'. Monaghan fled and Frisby cried, 'Oh, Dick, I'm stabbed.'

> My mother was dressing at the time of the scuffle. When she came out, Frisby was lying at Mr Fraser's corner. I saw Monaghan take the knife off the dressing-table. Monaghan jumped over the fence after they had taken Frisby to the hospital, and looked in at the window. My brother said, 'Hullo, Bill, there's nobody in.' Monaghan then came in, dressed himself in his best clothes, and tied up some blankets. He told us to go and look for our mother and bring her home. We did so and he was gone when we returned.

The court was then adjourned for the night, and the trial resumed at 10 o'clock the following morning, Friday 5 June. William Heyward continued his testimony, repeating some parts of his evidence from the previous day:

> It was after Monaghan said to my mother that he would strike

her that she went to bed ... Frisby and Gibbs were outside the house at this time. They came into the house by the front door, about three minutes after my mother went to bed. They came into the kitchen. Frisby came into our bedroom, when he gave us the nuts and pears, first lighting his pipe at the lamp. Gibbs followed him. Frisby asked Monaghan to have a drink, and he said, 'No, I don't drink anything strong at all.' At this time my mother was sitting on the side of the bed. She only had her petticoat on.

When Monaghan said to the visitors 'that they would oblige him if they went home, Frisby said he had as much right there as he had'. He and Gibbs left 'in a little time', with Monaghan following to shut the door after them. Sarah Heyward called from the bed, 'Don't quarrel with them, Bill, they are only my friends,' to which Monaghan replied, 'You dry up, I'll do what I please. They are nothing to you.' Frisby and Gibbs dragged Monaghan out onto the grass. 'He had the knife in his hand, and they were holding him by the wrists.' He then said, 'The first bloody man touches me, I'll put this knife in him!' When Frisby punched him on the arm, Monaghan said, 'You dare strike me again.' Frisby hit him twice on the back, then Monaghan 'made a drive at his chest with the knife' before running away. Under cross-examination William Heyward said he had never seen Frisby, Gibbs or Kerr before that night. He had never seen any of them visit his mother's house.

The previous Crown witnesses were recalled. Kerr denied seeing anything of the struggle, or Frisby and Gibbs pulling Monaghan outside. He saw no blows struck. Gibbs denied taking Monaghan by the wrists or pulling him onto the grass. Indeed, Gibbs denied almost all of William Heyward's testimony. He did not see the boy at the door or outside, and wondered how he could have seen anything from his bedroom.

Mr Justice Gresson then questioned Gibbs, who said he had not made any improper proposals to Mrs Heyward that evening: 'I did not offer her five shillings or any other sum, nor did Frisby in my presence, or to my knowledge.' But he did not sound any more convincing than Sarah Heyward.

After hearing the medical testimony from Dr Coward and Dr Powell, Duncan closed his case. Dr Foster had two more witnesses, who testified that Frisby had come to the bar of the White Horse Hotel two or three days after the stabbing and said he was getting better and would be all right in a day or two. He had a glass of port wine before returning to the hospital. The Crown prosecutor then produced a witness who had been in the same ward as Frisby and said he had never left his bed. Gibbs had claimed that he visited Frisby every day while he was in hospital and he had never been out.

Dr Foster's address to the jury argued that while there was no doubt that Monaghan had stabbed Frisby, there had been enough provocation to reduce the crime to manslaughter. Dr Foster thought young William Heyward had been the only satisfactory witness. He at least had been sober that night, whereas all the other witnesses had been drinking:

> The boy had been subjected to an extraordinarily long examina-
> tion, yet he had not contradicted himself in any material point;
> while his mother, though he did not believe she had committed
> wilful perjury, had given her evidence in a most blundering
> manner, so that it was absurd to suppose that she could have
> tutored him. He (Dr Foster) had not done so either, and Mona-
> ghan had not had any opportunity of doing so.

Gibbs, Kerr and Monaghan had given 'a very short account of a long evening', while the boy had been 'more explicit and probably more observing'. Because of his friendship with Frisby, Gibbs had done his best to present the case in a manner favourable to his friend, and to himself. They had been a long while on the road, and at the White Horse, with Mrs Heyward, yet none of them had given a convincing account of their movements.

By contrast, Monaghan had been 'beset with great difficulties in defending himself'. He had been unable to obtain evidence from the two passers-by who had witnessed the scuffle, as they could not be found. Dr Foster concluded that there was no doubt that Monaghan's home had been invaded by 'a set of persons who were not perfectly sober', who came into his bedroom and behaved in a familiar fashion with the woman with whom he was living. When they prevented him from correcting her and telling her to come inside, as he was legally justified in doing, he pushed Frisby away, who then struck him. Monaghan was holding the knife he had been using to cut tobacco, and in the heat of the moment stabbed Frisby, causing his death. Dr Foster contended that there was no intention to kill, merely to wound, and that the case was reducible to manslaughter done under circumstances of great provocation.

In reply, Duncan said that the evidence of Gibbs and Kerr seemed truthful, while that of Mrs Heyward was positively false, and the boy's was not entirely reliable. Frisby had gone to the house on an errand of charity, to give the children fruit and nuts, and had told Monaghan so. But when Mrs Heyward came to the door to talk to the men as they were leaving, Monaghan went back into the house and returned with a knife, and with malicious intent. Frisby had defended himself, but Monaghan had stabbed him close to the heart. Duncan contended that Monaghan had provoked Frisby, not the other way around, and that Monaghan had expressed an intention to use the knife. He asked the jury not to be led away by any feelings of compassion for the prisoner, but to do their duty and give their verdict according to the evidence.

In summing up, Gresson said he was pleased to see 'the unflagging attention which the jury had paid to this case', in which the life of a fellow human being was at stake. The questions to be answered were: Was the wound inflicted by the prisoner? If so, did it cause the death from a legal point of view? And, lastly, was the wound inflicted under such circumstances as would make the crime murder or could it be reduced to manslaughter? There was no doubt that the prisoner gave the blow, and the Crown did not have to prove whether the best possible treatment had been applied. Even if Frisby had left hospital and taken a glass of port on the Tuesday, that would not make his death any less the result of the blow. According to Dr Powell's evidence, Frisby was in danger from the first or second day. Gresson then quoted authorities to show what constituted murder and what manslaughter, and commented on the evidence. After retiring for only a short time, the jury returned with a verdict of manslaughter.

Although he agreed with the verdict, Gresson 'would not have been surprised if a different one had been brought in'. The jury had, however, taken a very merciful view of the case. He trusted that the prisoner would reflect on his past life while in prison, and, if spared to complete his sentence, would leave gaol a better man than he entered it. Monaghan was sentenced to four years' penal servitude.

His friends, however, started a petition on his behalf, suggesting that he had some loyal and faithful supporters, and after a long delay they were successful. Monaghan was pardoned by the governor on 9 February 1871 and immediately released from prison. The Canterbury *Police Gazette* described him as a sawyer, of medium build and fresh complexion, 5ft 10in in height (177cm) with grey eyes and auburn hair. He had a tattoo on his left arm, presumably of his initials, 'W.M.' Nothing more is known of him from police records, so his two and a half years in gaol may have made him resolve to keep out of trouble for the rest of his life.

CHAPTER EIGHT

A MAGISTERIAL MISCELLANY

Charles Christopher Bowen
(1830–1917), Godley's
secretary, inspector of
police, provincial treasurer,
joint owner of the *Lyttelton
Times*, resident magistrate
of Christchurch 1864–74,
Minister of Justice 1874–77,
and chief architect of the
Education Act of 1877.
Later vice-chancellor of the
University of New Zealand.

Alexander Turnbull Library,
PA coll 083

Christchurch's resident magistrate, Christopher Bowen, was regarded by some as too soft-hearted when it came to sentencing criminals, but the court reports show that he had no hesitation in punishing repeat offenders, and even those who had been driven to steal by desperation or destitution, with stiff fines. He must have had a great fund of human kindness to stay cheerful and optimistic. It would surely have been easy to become cynical when confronted with so much wrongdoing, deceit and deception, and sometimes sheer wickedness, yet Bowen remained well respected and much liked in the town. He belonged to many organisations, such as the Christchurch Club, the Canterbury Acclimatisation Society, the Rowing Club and the Jockey Club, so he spent much of his spare time in the company of respectable and law-abiding people, which may have counter-balanced the procession of drunkards, thieves and prostitutes with whom he spent his working day.

Sometimes the offenders had been too drunk to remember what they had done. This was often the case with prostitutes charged with disorderly behaviour and abusive language, but a case with a difference came before Bowen in 1868. On 9 July one Patrick McCabe was brought before Bowen for having been drunk on Papanui Road, entering a private house illegally and damaging private property there. The house belonged to Henry Webb, a prominent businessman whose servant, Edwin Henry, told the court that at 6 o'clock the night before he had heard someone rattling the kitchen windows, and when he went outside to investigate he found the prisoner, 'very drunk', trying to open them. When challenged, the man had replied that he was feeling cold and wanted a bed for the night. He then forced his way past Henry and went into the kitchen, where he knocked over several things and broke a window. He refused to leave when asked – the *Press* reported that he lay on the floor – and 'began to be disorderly', so the servant seized him and called his master.

When Bowen asked the man what he thought he had been doing, the prisoner said he knew nothing whatever of the matter. He had taken some cattle into Christchurch during the day, but had no recollection of how he came to be on Mr Webb's property. Inspector Pender said that McCabe was not the man's real name and that he was a farmer in Harewood Road called Sadler. (The *Press* stated that his real name was Kavanagh.) He had never been in court before and was known in the district as a respectable man. Bowen said that the offence was a very serious one, and he must deal severely with illegal entry and disorderly conduct in another man's home, but he would take into account the fact that Sadler had never been in trouble with the law before. He imposed a fine of 40s, and advised Sadler to pay at once for the damage he had caused, before Webb sued him.

It sounds as if the farmer had celebrated the sale of his cattle with a drink in a pub, where he probably fell victim to the custom of 'treating' or 'shouting rounds'. For someone unaccustomed to drinking in a pub, a group of convivial 'good fellows' could very quickly get a man drunk and fleece him of his money. Bowen had evidently taken a sympathetic view of the farmer's plight. The same offence committed by a known drunkard would almost certainly have resulted in a prison sentence.

Sometimes a claim for damages could backfire. In April 1868 a man called Richards was riding his mare from Christchurch towards Riccarton through Hagley Park when he collided with a horse and cart coming the other way, driven by a man called Hart. Both shafts of the cart were broken and the mare was killed. Richards was now claiming £40 as the value of his horse. He told the court that he was on the proper side of the road but did not see the cart coming because he was looking at the Maori encampment in Hagley Park. (This was where Maori stayed when they brought goods to town to sell in the Market Place.) Hart had demanded £3 from Richards for the repair of the shafts; as a compromise, Richards had offered not to ask anything for the mare if Hart dropped his claim. Hart refused and summoned him for £3 damages. The summons for the value of the shafts would now be decided by the outcome of the present case.

Under cross-examination in court in July Richards said that he was riding with his friend John Gammel, and that the collision had occurred at 6.30pm when it was almost dark. Gammel was riding on the wrong side of the road, and almost had to ride up on the footpath to avoid the cart. Gammel, called as a witness, confirmed Richards' testimony. Under further questioning he admitted that they had both had 'a glass or two', but denied that either of them had been intoxicated.

Hart, however, had two witnesses who had been riding on the cart with him. They confirmed that Hart had been on the correct side of the road, driving towards Christchurch at about 7 miles per hour, when they met the two horsemen galloping towards them. The road curved up from a gully at that point and they did not see the riders until they were almost upon the cart. The horses had swerved to go on either side of the cart, and Gammel had definitely ridden onto the footpath, but Richards' mare had impaled herself on one of the cart's shafts and died on the spot. Bowen said it was evident that the plaintiff was in the wrong, and there was no need to hear any further evidence. He gave judgement for the defendant, with costs, and Richards agreed to pay the £3 for the broken shafts.

Drink was also involved in another unusual case at the end of July 1868. Jacob Fitzenberger was charged with having been drunk and disorderly in a public house, and with wilful damage to private property. Constable Wilson told the court he had been called to the White Horse Hotel in Tuam Street at 2.30pm the previous day and there took custody of the prisoner, who was very drunk. The barman, Joseph Plank, said Fitzenberger had come in with another man and ordered a small bottle of champagne. When Plank had replied that they did not look like champagne customers, Fitzenberger's companion had said, 'Oh, he's come from a country where they drink nothing else but champagne, and so let him have it.' Plank complied and the friend drank his glass and left. Fitzenberger asked for another glass but the barman refused to serve him until the first bottle had been paid for, adding that he did not want any German loafers in his bar.

At this Fitzenberger became 'excited' and threatened to hit Plank with a pitcher. The barman quickly removed this, but Fitzenberger then 'seized the stone used for striking matches on, and retreating to the centre of the bar ... threw it with all his force'. Plank ducked and the stone sailed past him to hit a glass barrel full of Old Tom gin, and several other bottles beside it. The glass barrel contained about 5 gallons of spirits, worth about £10. The barman called a constable and Fitzenberger was taken into custody.

When asked what he had to say for himself, the prisoner did not deny the offence but 'pleaded drunkenness in extenuation'. He had been working on a fencing contract for a farmer at Leeston and had come into Christchurch to spend his wages. He was very willing to pay for the damage, but doubted that he had enough ready money, and asked to be allowed to go back to Leeston to earn enough to cover the amount. He was fined 10s for being drunk and advised to make arrangements to pay the value of the property he had destroyed. This was a fairly light sentence, but there had been an element of provocation and the damage had to some extent been accidental: the stone had obviously been intended for the barman rather than the gin.

Prizefighting was illegal in the 1860s but it was a popular pastime among the rougher elements of colonial society, mainly for the money that could be made from betting on the outcome, and even quite respectable citizens would join a crowd to watch the fun. After receiving a tip-off on 29 July 1898 Police Detective Harry Feast proceeded – how else do policemen move? – out to Riccarton Road, where he found a crowd of 40–50 men gathered on the road reserve near the Plough Inn. He recognised a number of them, including the notorious cabbie Christopher Dalwood, who was often before the magistrate for minor offences such as leaving his cab unattended while he nipped into a pub for a drink. One of the men, James Gatherer, came over to Feast and started 'chaffing' him: 'I think he said the fight was only for love. I said it had better be stopped as it would not do.' The crowd then moved off towards Riccarton Racecourse, and Feast followed, but by the time he caught up with them the fight was over and the principals were riding off: 'The people were scattered when I arrived, but I should think there were about fifty.'

As a result of Detective Feast's enquiries, Stephen Moon and Patrick McGuire were later arrested and charged with taking part as principals in a prizefight, and six other men, including Christopher

Dalwood, were charged with aiding and abetting. They came before the Magistrate's Court on 4 August. Bowen was on leave so the case was heard by Dr Alexander Back and Thomas Maude as JPs.

Saddler Thomas Haskett of Tuam Street, Christchurch, was a key witness for the prosecution, although he 'seemed very disinclined to give evidence'. He had heard there was a fight in progress on Riccarton Road, and followed the crowd to the racecourse:

> I saw the prisoners McGuire and Moon, who were sparring. They had no gloves on and must have been fighting. It was nearly over when I arrived. I could not say how many rounds were fought after my arrival. I have seen men fighting before. The men were striking each other. Moon was bleeding, but he was marked before the fight. I did not see a knock down, but they caught hold of each other, wrestled, and fell. When they got up they sparred again. This would be a round. I saw two or three rounds.
>
> I believed it to be a drunken spree ... I heard they were sparring to decide who was the best man. There were seconds and a bottle holder. I saw accused Gatherer holding Moon on his knee. Dalwood was in the ring, and I saw Turner holding a watch in his hand. I heard him call out time, and I suppose he was the timekeeper. When time was called, the men were seated or standing against the knees of their seconds. Gatherer was one of the seconds. I saw Spinks in the ring ... Someone said the police were coming, and the crowd disappeared, Moon and McGuire riding away. The fight was not concluded. There was between forty and fifty persons present. There was no row, nor much noise during the fight.

James Gatherer was questioned closely about his role in the affair, but claimed not to have seen any betting or money changing hands, which probably made most people in court smile in disbelief. He admitted going out with the others in a cart in the expectation of seeing a fight, as he had heard Moon say that he would be fighting McGuire that day:

I believe Moon had one black eye ... before the fight at the Racecourse. I could not say whether both were black. I have seen prize fights before, but they had ropes round. There were no ropes around the ring at the Racecourse, which was only formed by the people standing around. The rounds that were fought would perhaps occupy perhaps 4 or 5 minutes each. None of them lasted a quarter of an hour. A minute was allowed to elapse between each round.

James Alfred Selfe, who described himself as a gentlemen residing in Christchurch, had seen the crowd gather and went over to see what was happening. He identified Moon and McGuire as the principals, and thought they had fought 15 or 16 short rounds before the crowd scattered at the arrival of the police. He confirmed Gatherer's testimony that there were no ropes, just a circle of grass surrounded by the crowd. He also supported Gatherer's claim that no bets were made, as he did not hear any being laid. He identified all of the others accused, but thought that some of them took no active part, merely watching from the crowd.

Without firm testimony of betting, this affray had to be regarded merely as a drunken brawl that had attracted a crowd. The JPs were not impressed by the attempts of the accused to make excuses for each other, and fined Moon and McGuire £5 each, with sureties of £25 each for their 'peaceable behaviour' over the next 12 months. Turner and Gatherer were fined £2 each for aiding and abetting. The others were dismissed with a warning that prizefighting was illegal, and that if they were involved in future in a fight where money changed hands, they would be liable to 'severe punishment'.

Christopher Bowen returned from leave and took up his magisterial duties again before the end of August 1868. One of the first cases he had to consider was a charge of wilful and malicious destruction of property against three men, Thomas McKay, Ben Perry and

John McGuinness. Constable Pratt had arrested the trio in the early hours of that morning, after being called to Joseph Hadley's house in Colombo Street. Hadley told the constable that he had been woken about 1.30am by a lodger who said someone was destroying his fence. Hadley looked out of the front window and saw the three men leaning on his fence, 'laughing and making a great noise'. When he went outside he found that the fence had been pushed over, and some shingles had been taken from the roof of his cottage. When he set off to look for a policeman, McKay had followed him with a shingle in his hand, asking if his life was insured and threatening to kill him. Hadley told him to go away, but McKay 'persisted in following him and using threatening language'. At last Hadley met Constable Pratt, who soon found the men nearby, drunk and incapable.

Mrs Hadley gave corroborative evidence, adding that several windows had been broken in the vicinity a few nights before, though she could not say that these men had been responsible. Each of the accused admitted the offence. McKay 'pleaded in extenuation that they had taken a glass too much' and were merely 'larking'. The fence had been knocked down when he pushed Perry against it.

Inspector Pender told the court that there had been a great deal of drunken 'larking' lately and that a lot of property had been damaged or destroyed as a result. Magistrate Bowen said that drink was 'no excuse for such conduct, which could not be tolerated'. He fined the prisoners 20s each and ordered them to make good the damage they had done.

Sometimes the witnesses proved more difficult than the accused. The very next case that day concerned a Leeston storekeeper named James F. Douglas, who was facing three charges of selling beer without a licence. A witness, local labourer William Boyce, admitted to having beer at the store, along with some biscuits and cheese, on 24 July. Douglas, in his own defence, said that he had lost his licence, having missed the date for its renewal, but had hopes of regaining it, and in the meantime he supplied ordinary refreshments to travellers with food, including the drink with the price of the meal. He said that he was in the habit of giving his customers a glass of beer 'in order to keep them together until he got a renewal of his licence'. Bowen was not impressed by this excuse but said he would hear the other two charges before giving judgement.

The witness for the second charge had not appeared, so that was adjourned until he could be found. The third charge involved a man called Sutherland, who proved to be a difficult witness. On being put into the witness box he said he had forgotten his Christian name, and for some time refused to be sworn, claiming that he had no religious convictions. Finally he agreed to swear the oath, but continued to conduct himself 'in such a strange manner' that Bowen asked Inspector Pender if anything was wrong with the witness's mind. Pender said not, and remarked that he had been a witness in court several times in civil cases, at which the witness piped up, 'Yes, very civil, certainly!'

When Bowen asked him where he lived, Sutherland replied that he had no home and lived anywhere. Another attempt was made to get him to give his evidence but he proved very evasive. He could not remember being at the defendant's store on the day in question, nor could he remember speaking about it to the constable. All that could be extracted from him was that he occasionally had a meal at the store, but usually took water with it. The magistrate had to caution him several times, and finally ordered him to stand down until the first charge was dealt with.

Though Douglas claimed to have conducted his house in a proper manner when he had a licence, Bowen had a longer memory, and recalled having fined him once before for a breach of the licensing ordinance. On the first charge he fined the storekeeper £5 and insisted that it be paid that same day or he would be sent to prison. The second charge would be adjourned to the following week, and the third charge 'would fall to the ground' for lack of evidence.

The witness Sutherland was then recalled, and Bowen told him that he had either not taken his oath seriously or was of unsound mind. He would be allowed the benefit of the doubt and be discharged, but if he behaved in a similar fashion again in a court of law he would be either charged with contempt of court or committed to the lunatic asylum at Sunnyside.

Cases of theft or larceny were common in the Magistrate's Court, but rarely do we get a glimpse of the motivation behind such crimes. Early in September 1868 Bowen heard Detective Harry Feast giving evidence against one William John Jones, alias Jonas, who was charged with stealing a parcel containing a pair of boots and gaiters from a cart in Cathedral Square on the previous Saturday afternoon. Feast said he had first noticed Jones in Preece's Saleyards, going from cart to cart and turning over the straw to see what might be underneath. After this he did the same with a number of carts and traps parked in a corner of Cathedral Square. He then went and stood on the footpath near Matson's buildings, but in a few moments he returned to one of the carts, took out a parcel and walked quickly away into Hereford Street. Feast followed the man, arrested him and took him to the lockup in the Market Place. He then went and found the owner of the cart, a Kaiapoi farmer named Donald Coutts, who identified the boots as those he had previously purchased at George Gould's Cookham House on Colombo Street. The value of the items in the parcel was 25s.

In court Jones declined to make any statement at first, and Inspector Pender told the court that the prisoner had previously been convicted in Sydney. Jones then explained that he had been arrested for issuing some bills for goods worth a considerable sum of money, but he had been freed on a technicality after spending three months in custody. That had been more than eight years before, and since then he had 'occupied a good position in society'. He had kept several hotels, and for the last 18 months had lived at the Riccarton Hotel. He had been all over the country looking for work, offering his wife's services as a domestic servant as well as his own, for 10s a week, but with no success.

He had nothing to say about the charge of larceny, except that he had 'not a bit of coal or food in the house, and his family could not do without'. He hoped, whatever was done with him, that provision would be made for his wife and children. Magistrate Bowen said that he could not take the last point into consideration, as the robbery had been 'a most deliberate one'. There had been many such crimes of late, and an example had to be made. He then sentenced Jones to six months' imprisonment with hard labour, which seems rather harsh for the theft of a pair of boots. One wonders how his wife managed to feed the children while he was in prison.

The desperation of an unemployed man with a family to feed can readily be understood, but theft by someone in employment and in a position of trust was far less excusable, and was usually punished much more harshly. Yet one such case in October 1868 ended with a much lighter sentence than that of the unfortunate William Jones, and may help to explain why some people thought Bowen too soft-hearted, especially when a woman was involved.

Catherine Gilchrist, 'a respectably dressed female', was charged with stealing various items of clothing from her former employer, Gilbert Butler, who lived in Manchester Street. She was now living as a servant in the house of one Mr Farmer on Lincoln Road, near the railway crossing. Detective Harry Feast, who had received a tip-off, interviewed Catherine Gilchrist at the Farmer house. He searched her basket and there found the crinoline, muslin, hat and ribbon that Butler had reported missing; he later identified them as his wife's clothing. When Feast arrested Gilchrist, 'she begged very hard to be let off, and said that she would not do it again'.

Because Gilchrist declined to say anything in her defence it was left to Police Sergeant Pardy to inform the court about her previous life. She had emigrated to Canterbury from Donegal the previous July in the *Lancashire Witch*, along with a number of assisted single women who had since shown themselves to be 'of a very low class'. They were anxious to find steady employment in a new land, but some of the rowdy younger women soon became well known to the Christchurch police as prostitutes. Gilchrist was not one of them, however. The Canterbury *Police Gazette* described her as a short (157cm), stout, Irish 18-year-old, with grey eyes and light brown hair. Sergeant Pardy assured the court that Gilchrist had been in several situations as a servant, and had 'a very respectable character'.

Bowen addressed the prisoner with a stern warning that stealing by servants or persons occupying positions of trust 'was a very serious matter and deserving of severe punishment'. However, in view of her good character and lack of previous convictions he would pass a light sentence in the hope that she would 'start on a better course of life'. Gilchrist 'earnestly promised that she would'. The magistrate then sentenced her to one month's imprisonment. Sadly, that conviction and imprisonment would have demolished whatever good character she had hitherto claimed. On being released she would have found it very hard, if not impossible, to find domestic work again in Christchurch, at least with a respectable family. Her best course would have been to move to another city where she was not known, to make a fresh start.

By contrast, the notorious prostitute Emma Craigie, who now had 16 previous convictions, had been in court so often that she treated it and the magistrate with a familiarity that bordered on contempt. On 14 November 1868 she appeared yet again before Magistrate Bowen charged with having been drunk and disorderly, and with having exposed herself in a public place. Constable Wallace testified to her behaviour, which she 'very emphatically denied'. Bowen said wearily that he had no doubt about her guilt, and must send her back to prison. He had let her off a similar charge only a few days before, in the hope that she would better behave herself, but his leniency had not produced the desired improvement.

The fact was, Bowen continued, letting her be at liberty was bad for herself and a nuisance to the public, which he would no longer permit. At this Emma Craigie spoke up: 'Oh, if you don't believe me, give me 12 months, I don't care.' Bowen may have been tempted, but said that he would, at all events, send her to gaol for six months with hard labour. Emma Craigie's response was to drop a mock curtsey and respond, 'Thank you, your Worship.'

CHAPTER NINE

ELIZA BENNETT: 'COVERED WITH BLOOD'

A BRUTAL FELLOW.
Policeman – 'Now, Mum. What's the matter?'
Injured Female – 'If you please Mister, I want to give my wretch of a 'usband in charge. He is always a knocking of me down and stampin' on me!'

John Leech, *Four Hundred Humorous Illustrations*, 2nd edn, 1862

About 4pm on Saturday 14 May 1870 fellmonger John Pepperell was approaching his home in Montreal Street South, Sydenham, when he heard the voice of a neighbour across the street, Edwin Bennett, raised 'in loud and angry tones'. Bennett was 'swearing violently' and saying that he would send someone to hell. Pepperell heard blows and thought Bennett was hitting the table with his stock whip. Next door to the Bennett house, Janet Lusk heard the noise of a quarrel and the smashing of crockery. Edwin Bennett was shouting 'You're drunk!', and Eliza Bennett was denying this. Bennett then said she was a bad woman, and all went quiet.

A few minutes later Mrs Lusk saw Edwin Bennett come out of his house and wash his hands in a bucket of water: 'I saw blood on his hands.' He then came over to Mrs Lusk and calmly asked how much they owed for milk. She said it was not quite a week. He gave her a shilling, remarking bitterly, 'I cannot go away from home but I find her drunk.' A quarter of an hour later he got on his horse and rode off.

With more than a little trepidation, Janet Lusk knocked at her neighbour's door. Eliza Bennett answered but when Mrs Lusk asked her what was the matter she would not say, and shut the door in her face. Frightened by Mrs Bennett's bloodstained appearance, Mrs Lusk went to seek help, and sent a boy to fetch the police. A neighbour forced the door open and they found Mrs Bennett sitting in a chair, covered with blood and water: 'She was quite wet.' It looked as if someone had started to clean up the blood but had abandoned the attempt. Mrs Lusk bathed the wound on her head, which was bleeding, took off her wet clothes, put dry clothes on her and put her to bed. Dr William Deamer happened to be passing by and was called in. He said the injuries were serious and she would have to be taken to the hospital.

Then Sergeant McKnight arrived and was taken through to the bedroom. He saw Mrs Bennett lying on a bed, with her head between two pillows. As he later testified, 'There was a large clot of blood about her head, and blood was oozing out from wounds at the back of her head. She appeared to be very weak ... The floor of the front room was covered with water and blood; lumps of clotted blood were on the floor, and the walls for about four feet high were marked with blood.' He also noticed blood on the front door, the fireplace and the window.

McKnight found a broom handle in the front room, broken in three pieces. He also found a meat cleaver. Mrs Bennett said she had been struck on the head with a broom handle: 'She was so weak that

I had to put my ear down close to her to hear what she said.' With the help of some neighbours, the sergeant took Mrs Bennett to the hospital in a cab.

Mrs Lusk later told the Magistrate's Court that Eliza Bennett bled a great deal before being taken away by the sergeant: 'I saw bread and dough on the table; there was a number of broken articles lying about. I think Mrs Bennett had been drinking. She smelt of beer, but I do not think she was intoxicated.' Mrs Lusk later added in the Supreme Court that she had smelt a strong smell of drink when she went into the house. There was no alcohol to be seen, and no tumbler on the table, but on three previous occasions she knew Mrs Bennett had been drinking, 'from the smell and her manner of talking'. But she had never seen her drunk.

At the hospital Mrs Bennett was admitted by the house surgeon, Dr Henry Horsford Prins. He later told the Supreme Court jury that she was in a state of exhaustion from loss of blood, with a black eye, a sprained wrist and several bruises on her body. There were two serious wounds on her head: one at the back of the head, which was still bleeding, and a longer gash on her forehead. Her life would have been in danger if the wound on the back of her head had not been sutured and dressed. She was then out of danger, but remained in hospital for several weeks.

Edwin Bennett was soon found by the police, and Inspector Pender charged him with a violent assault with the intent to do his wife grievous bodily harm. He first appeared before Christopher Bowen in the Magistrate's Court on 27 May 1870. Eliza Bennett was brought to the courthouse from the hospital and allowed to remain seated while giving her evidence:

> I am the wife of the prisoner. My husband was away from home
> for a short time during the early part of this month. He returned
> on Saturday, the 14th, at about 4 pm. He left his horse in the
> yard, and came into the house. I was making some bread at the
> time, and when I saw him I said, 'Oh, papa, you have come back
> sooner than I expected.' He was just outside the door then, and

made some reply, but I did not hear it. In a moment afterwards
he struck me with the broom handle on the head ... I did not
fall from the first blow, but he struck me many more times, and
I ultimately fell from the effects of them. Before falling I put
up my hand, saying 'That's enough,' and he answered, 'You'll do
better without me.'

After she fell, Bennett struck her several more times on the head,
shoulders and left arm: 'The broom handle was broken as it is now
by the blows.' Eliza Bennett 'became insensible, and remained so for
several minutes'. When taken to hospital, she had to be lifted into a
cab. 'The clothes found in the house are mine. I bled very much. My
husband did not strike me with anything but the broom handle. I
cannot say how the blood came to be on the window, door and walls,
but I bled about an hour and a half before being removed.'

Edwin Bennett declined to make any statement. Indicted for
having 'feloniously, unlawfully and maliciously wounded one Eliza
Bennett, his wife', he was formally committed to take his trial at the
next session of the Supreme Court. That session opened on 8 June
1870, before Mr Justice Gresson. Bennett pleaded not guilty to the
charge of assault and inflicting grievous bodily harm. He said he
would conduct his own defence.

After hearing the testimony of Sergeant McKnight, the judge
asked the registrar to show him the indictment. Prosecutor Thomas
Duncan had indicted the prisoner under a section that treated the
offence as a misdemeanour, but the registrar had inserted the word
'feloniously'. Gresson said he would let the case go on, but if there
was a conviction he would take the opinion of his brother judges
on this technicality. A felony automatically carried heavier penalties
than a misdemeanour.

Eliza Bennett, 'who sobbed bitterly', repeated the gist of her previous statement in the Magistrate's Court, though instead of bread
she claimed to be making currant cakes for her children when her
husband returned home on 14 May. Questioned by him, Mrs Bennett proceeded to deny all his allegations:

I did not come to the door when you returned on Saturday. The children were not outside the house crying for bread when I went home. I had given the children their dinner a short time before. I am not aware that you brought the children down to buy them some cakes. There was a fire under the oven when you came home. The oven is close to the fire. I didn't see a saddle with you. I was not sitting asleep in a chair when you came in; I was standing alongside a table, making the cakes. I did not lift a stool to throw at you. I had no time to do anything, as you gave me a blow the moment you came in. I had no liquor that day. I am quite sure that I had taken neither beer, wine, nor spirits that day. I didn't go into Smith's of the Crown, that day, and change £1 and take away a quart of beer.

She had signed the pledge about a year ago, and kept it until her husband insisted that she drink a glass of beer with him in February. 'You brought beer home many times in your pocket after you had taken the pledge.'

You had never to wait until Sunday morning to get a clean shirt before you could go out anywhere. I never ironed the children's clothes on a Sunday morning before sending them to [Sunday] school. I may have turned their clothes [inside out] on one or two occasions, but not in a general way. The only drink I had was a glass of brandy, which was brought and given to me by someone – I don't recollect whom – after I was beaten.

I did not go out of the house after I was beaten until I was taken to the hospital. I am quite sure I was not at the A1 [Hotel] on the 14th. I was not from my home on the Friday or Saturday, except to fetch water, until I was taken to the hospital. There were two half-crowns and a shilling on the table when you came in. I had earned the money by sewing while you were away. I had not 11s in my hand besides. I know nothing about your going to the butcher's, paying a bill, and bringing the receipt back.

Janet Lusk and John Pepperell then repeated the evidence they had given in the Magistrate's Court, adding a few minor details under questioning by the foreman of the jury and the defendant. Pepperell responded to the latter's questions by stating: 'I did not see you strike your wife. I didn't see your children crying outside the house. You got home before me.'

Dr Prins repeated exactly his previous testimony, but in response to the defendant's questions admitted that if Mrs Bennett had fallen and hit her head on the edge of a box it would very likely have produced a wound like that on the back of her head. He also admitted that taking a stool out of her hand might sprain her wrist if she resisted.

This closed the Crown's case, and Edwin Bennett then spoke in his own defence. He maintained that when he got home on the Saturday afternoon two of the children were outside crying, and when he got inside he found his wife drunk in a chair. There was no fire in the oven. He went out to buy the children some cakes, and when he returned his wife jumped up, but then stumbled and fell, striking her head against a box and cutting the back of her head. He claimed that she then took up a stool to threaten him, and that when he wrested it from her, her wrist was sprained. The other wound had, he said, been made by Mrs Bennett herself when she tried to throw a quart pot half full of beer at him, and it broke on her head.

The judge summed up, and the jury retired for about an hour, returning with a verdict of 'Guilty, and a recommendation to mercy'. When Gresson enquired about this the foreman replied that the jury believed there could be some extenuating circumstances in connection with the 'drinking habits of his wife. He might have received some provocation.' The judge directed that the prisoner be taken down, as he was not then prepared to pass sentence, and the court moved on to more mundane matters such as horse-stealing, forgery and indecent assault.

A week later, on 16 June, Edwin Bennett again took his place at the bar of the court for sentencing. Although, as Gresson said, he had been 'convicted upon very clear evidence of a very heinous offence', because he had been undefended by counsel the judge had felt it his duty to 'act in a certain degree as your counsel' regarding the technical point over the indictment, and had asked for a Court of Appeal opinion. Until that was received, judgement would be postponed. If Edwin Bennett could pay £500 bail 'and two sureties in £250 each' he could stay out of gaol in the meantime. Bennett could not find such a large sum of money, or any sureties, and was taken to the Lyttelton Gaol.

The Court of Appeal acted with unusual promptness and in late July declared Bennett discharged because of the change in wording from the original indictment. The police then brought another charge of inflicting grievous bodily harm, this time properly worded, and Bennett appeared before Magistrate Bowen on 6 August. However, the police had not done all their paperwork and he was remanded in custody until the following week, when Thomas Joynt, appearing for Bennett, asked whether the magistrate intended dealing with the case summarily under the Offences Against Persons Act. Bowen replied that he would not be justified in doing so in view of the Court of Appeal decision. He would therefore deal with the case in the same manner as before. All the evidence previously given against Bennett was repeated, and he was committed to take his trial at the next session of the Supreme Court.

Bennett again appeared before Mr Justice Gresson on 8 September, facing two charges, one of unlawful and malicious wounding and a second of inflicting grievous bodily harm. Once again Bennett chose to represent himself, and pleaded not guilty. He then challenged five of the jurors, and the Crown prosecutor challenged another. Henry Leake was chosen foreman of the jury.

The same evidence was presented as in the previous trial. In his defence Bennett said that his wife was continually drunk, and that she had fallen down and struck her head against a box. In summing up, Mr Justice Gresson told the jury that if they believed the prisoner had inflicted the injuries on his wife, even supposing she had been the greatest drunkard to enter a public house, Bennett had no justification in law for assaulting her.

The jury retired, and after a short absence returned a guilty verdict on the second count. When asked if he had anything to say,

Bennett said he hoped the judge would take into consideration the amount of time he had been kept in prison. Gresson agreed, and sentenced him to 18 months with hard labour.

Some may regard this as a harsh sentence, destroying the reputation of a man with no previous convictions, but Bennett had come close to killing his wife in a fit of rage. If she had bled to death, as might have happened if Mrs Lusk had not had the courage to go and see how her neighbour was, he would have faced the death penalty. The first jury obviously had some sympathy for him, especially if he went away on business and came home to find his children neglected and starving while their mother spent the housekeeping money on beer. How often this had happened was not made clear in the evidence presented, but the fact that they had both signed the pledge suggests a willingness to deal with Eliza Bennett's drinking problem. Why he would then tempt her to drink beer with him is a puzzle, and the fact that he himself continued to drink himself must tend to diminish our sympathy. Nobody seems to have asked if he had been drinking that Saturday afternoon. Eliza Bennett may have been drinking more than she was willing to admit – alcoholics are notorious for self-deception – but she may have been the victim of a husband's rage fuelled by exasperation and one drink too many. It was fortunate for her that he had seized the broom handle and not the meat cleaver.

CHAPTER TEN

THE LONDON RESTAURANT FIRE OF 1870

Henry Barnes Gresson
(1809–1901), lawyer,
colonist, judge. In 1857 he
was appointed a judge with
jurisdiction over the whole
South Island (later reduced
to Nelson and Canterbury)
and settled in Christchurch
in 1859. He held the first
court on the West Coast, at
Hokitika, in 1865. Gresson
retired in 1875 and farmed
at Woodend, north of
Christchurch.

Alexander Turnbull Library,
½-008039-F

Fires were a common occurrence in early Christchurch. This was not surprising, considering that most of the buildings were wooden and became tinder-dry in summer, especially after a spell of hot nor'west winds. But insurance companies were naturally suspicious when the same premises were visited by fire twice within a short period. Insurance fraud was a great temptation to publicans and shopkeepers when times were hard, as we saw with the fire and murder in the Market Place in 1868 that led to the execution of John

138

Densley Swales. That event had made the Christchurch police all the more alert to possible cases of insurance fraud by arson.

One of the city's most memorable examples occurred in 1870, when two respectable Methodist women appeared before the Supreme Court charged with setting fire to the London Restaurant in Cashel Street with the intent to defraud two insurance companies. The restaurant was a small establishment, occupying what had been built as a two-storey shop between William Pratt's drapery store (soon to become J. Ballantyne's Dunstable House) and its rival clothing store on the Colombo Street corner, Waterloo House, built by Thomas Brass. This part of town had been the scene of a disastrous fire in 1864, and Pratt now protected his premises with a tall brick firewall along his right-of-way. This wall had not long been finished when the London Restaurant went up in flames on 10 March 1870. Yet this was not the first fire on these premises.

The restaurant had been established by John Patterson in the new premises built after the 1864 fire. He leased the building and lived upstairs with his wife, Margaret. Her friend, Miss Emily Jane Williams, also lived with them from 1868. George Gould, as agent for the owner, Lawson Cape, had insured the building for £500 with the Pacific Insurance Company. In 1868 the *Star* carried regular advertisements for the London Restaurant, offering meals at all hours, private rooms for suppers, 'wines and ales of the best brands' and accommodation for a few boarders at 'moderate terms'. One speciality of the house was Welsh rarebit for one shilling between 7 and 11pm. In February 1869 a new advertisement appeared, offering counter lunches and suppers with a glass of ale, and tea and coffee at all hours. Weekly board was also available. In March a series of smaller advertisements offered 'Good Accommodation for Gentlemen'. In April 'A Select Supper and Ball' was to be held in the 'New Café' at the London Restaurant in honour of the visit to Christchurch of HRH the Duke of Edinburgh; tickets cost 5s.

However, John Patterson died in mid-1869 and his widow struggled to make the business pay. She advertised for a new cook and housemaid, and was still advertising for the housemaid a month later. She had decided to apply for a full public house licence, to replace her existing wine and beer licence. Then somebody complained to the city council about the smell from the drain behind the restaurant, and the inspector of nuisances found that the stench came from an old decayed wooden culvert. Margaret Patterson was advised to replace it with an iron or tile pipe. This was in September 1869. That same month her application for a public house licence was refused, opposed by the neighbours on the grounds that there were already far too many pubs in the central city.

Adding to her woes, the lease expired on 18 September and George Gould had given her notice to vacate the premises that day, as he had another tenant ready to occupy. Mrs Patterson had previously complained about the rent, saying she could not afford it. Her lease had a clause enabling her to extend it for another two years if she desired, and Gould reluctantly agreed to this, reducing her rent by £1 a week, from £260 to £200 a year.

Towards the end of November 1869 Mrs Patterson employed a woman named Margaret Regan as a general servant or maid of all work, combining the duties of cook and housemaid. She later testified that the business was really being run by Mrs Patterson's friend, Miss Williams, who supervised the bar and café and looked after the takings. The two women often went off into the country after church on Sundays, taking two carpet-bags with them.

Margaret Regan later told the court of some strange goings-on in the first week of December 1869. Several bags, quite heavy and bulky, and large boxes were taken out of a private room and loaded into a cab. One bag was marked with Miss Williams's name. Mrs Patterson explained that she was not in good health and was going into the country for a few days. Margaret Regan noticed that various items vanished from the restaurant about this time and did not reappear, including a clock and a large portrait of the late Mr Patterson. She wondered if Mrs Patterson was taking things away for safekeeping elsewhere.

Then on Saturday 11 December 1869 Emily Williams told Margaret Regan that she could have the Sunday off work. That evening, a cabman named Henry Dodd was called to take Mrs Patterson out to Shakespeare's Hotel in Halswell, on the way to Lake Ellesmere. He recalled loading several packages and a heavy carpet-bag into the cab. Emily Williams was not present. They had driven only a short distance from the hotel when Mrs Patterson asked him to turn around and return to Christchurch. They got back about 11pm, and he put the bag and packages back inside the restaurant.

Margaret Regan had enjoyed her day off and returned to the London Restaurant about 9pm on the Sunday, to find the place in great disorder. There had been a fire: 'The things were all upset in the café. The mantelpiece was burnt down, and the large mirror also.' There were two men with Miss Williams, who said that she had been in the house all day reading, and had gone out briefly, only to return and find the café ablaze. She assumed that the cat had jumped onto the clothes-horse and knocked the clothes into the fire. A passing police constable had noticed the flames and helped to extinguish them. But Mrs Patterson insisted that someone had broken in and deliberately started the fire.

Margaret Regan left Mrs Patterson's employ on 12 January 1870, having been there about two months. Before she left she helped to take a double bed downstairs and put it in the bedroom behind the dining room. Mrs Patterson said there was a gentleman coming to stay, but he slept there for only two nights: 'Mrs Patterson had lodgers in the house whenever she could get them – not very often.' On Margaret Regan's last day of service she saw Mrs Patterson take several bags away and return with them empty. She thought that perhaps Miss Williams was leaving the house.

After the December fire Mrs Patterson made a claim on her insurance policy with the Royal Insurance Company for repairs and replacement of the mirror. She was paid £39 14s. The policy was for a sum of £500 on household furniture, personal effects, the piano and stock-in-trade of the London Restaurant. John Flavel was a cabinet-maker who did the repairs in the café. Mrs Patterson also asked him to put strong bolts on the doors leading to the back passage and bedroom. She told him, 'That was the door they broke into on the Sunday night of the fire.' Flavel also bored holes in a wall for new gas pipes to service a boiler on the bar for heating water for tea and coffee.

Mrs Patterson had failed in her bid for a publican's licence, but was apparently exploring other ways to improve the business early in 1870. On 14 January the *Star* carried an advertisement calling for tenders 'for alterations and erecting a billiard room' at the London Restaurant, closing on 1 February. It is not known whether she had any tenders, or whether the work was ever started.

There were many witnesses to the fire that destroyed the London Restaurant in the early hours of 10 March 1870. The alarm was first raised by Police Sergeant John Pratt, who was on duty near the Bank of New Zealand on the Hereford–Colombo streets corner when he saw smoke rising above Cashel Street about 3.20am. He ran towards the Cashel Street corner, shouting 'Fire!', thus rousing many of the inhabitants of the central city. The smoke was coming from the roof of the London Restaurant. The front door was locked but he put his shoulder to the door below the glass pane and forced it open.

There was no one in the house. When Pratt, in his words, 'forced in another door leading from the front shop to a passage', he saw a fire on the staircase on the right-hand side, just past the door he had forced open. The fire was 'at an angle on the staircase, about seven feet from the ground. The sides of the staircase and the steps were on fire. There was no fire below the stairs. The flames were reaching for about three feet from the steps up the side of the wall.' He then headed along a passage into the café, where he saw fire on the top of the piano – some papers that were burning the wall – at the far end of the room. 'That was all I noticed to be on fire in the café.' He pointed out that there was 'no connection between the two fires – the one on the piano, and the other on the stairs'.

He knocked the papers off the piano and tried to extinguish them but could not. He then returned through the passage leading from the café and entered the dining room. 'There was no smoke or fire there.' Pratt crossed the dining room and entered a small lean-to bedroom containing an undisturbed double bed: 'There was a quilt and sheets on it; they were laid back at the top, ready for a person to lie in the bed.' The window of the room, which led into a passage at the back of the house that gave access to Colombo Street, was open. The sergeant did not see any door from the lean-to into the yard. After trying unsuccessfully to open a back door leading from the dining room into this uncovered passage, he went back through the dining room to the front of the house and out onto Cashel Street, then ran around to Colombo Street and along a passage that led to the back of the restaurant. It was there that he found Mrs Patterson and Miss Williams:

> They were standing still. Mrs Patterson spoke to me, and asked me where she could go to dress herself. She had her petticoats on then. Miss Williams was completely dressed. She had all her clothes on – hat and chignon also. Mrs Patterson had a bundle of clothes on her arm. Before I met them I did not hear any alarm of fire from them.

Sergeant Pratt left the women and attempted to go back into the café, but the fire above the piano was now as high as the ceiling. Then he saw Albert Bradwell in the lean-to bedroom, and asked him what he was doing. Bradwell answered that Mrs Patterson had sent him to look for some jewellery. They searched the dressing table but found nothing.

Albert Bradwell later told the court that he lived on Colombo Street with his father, also named Albert, and was woken by the noise of someone banging on a door. He then saw the glare of a fire from the direction of the London Restaurant and ran downstairs and across the street. He saw Mrs Patterson and Miss Williams standing in the alleyway, 'trembling violently'. Mrs Patterson was saying, 'Oh, dear me! What shall I do? Where shall I go to?' Bradwell took them both into his house. Mrs Patterson was in her nightdress, and 'appeared to be putting on a skirt'. She was bare-headed and had some clothes in her arms. Miss Williams 'had the appearance of being fully dressed', Bradwell noticed: 'She had a skirt and jacket on, and her hat likewise.' When he asked Margaret Patterson if he could save anything she said that there was some jewellery and valuables on the dressing table in the back bedroom, so he went back to look for them, and thus met Sergeant Pratt.

Another neighbour woken by Sergeant Pratt's shouts of 'Fire!' was Fire Brigade Superintendent William Harris, who lived on Lichfield Street just behind the London Restaurant. He ran around to the Colombo Street alleyway just as Mrs Patterson and Miss Williams were walking towards Albert Bradwell's house. Harris found the fire well established at the rear, and then rushed to the Cashel Street entrance. Constable Willis had now joined Sergeant Pratt, after vigorously ringing the fire bell.

Extinguisher arrived first in Cashel Street, and even as the men were unrolling their hoses the Hook and Ladder Company and the old No. 2 manual engine *Dreadnought* drew up. Volunteers from the fire police also started to appear, and got busy removing furniture and stock from the London Restaurant and the shops on either side. Harris sent the manual pump around to the alleyway, where the men soon directed a jet of water onto the rear of the restaurant, but *Extinguisher* had only enough pressure to run one hose instead of its usual two. Harris sent the rest of its crew to help the Hook and Ladder Company pull down fences and outbuildings at the rear, to prevent the fire from spreading. He hoped to confine the fire between Pratt's brick wall and Brass's drapery store, but Marcus Sandstein's jewellery shop soon caught alight, and flames were seen inside Brass's store. There was a light southerly breeze blowing. Within ten minutes all three buildings were fully involved, and after half an hour the walls fell in before the fire was brought under control. Showers of sparks had threatened buildings on the north side of Cashel Street but buckets of water and wet blankets saved them. Brass's premises and the London Restaurant were gutted.

Sandstein was insured for £700, and Brass for £4000, though the latter claimed that he had lost over £5000 worth of stock in the fire. In addition to her £500 insurance policy with the Royal, Mrs Patterson also had furniture cover of £250 with the Australian and Alliance Insurance Company. At the inquest held before Dr Coward on 11 March she claimed her total losses amounted to £1000, as she had lost £150 in cash along with some valuable plate and jewellery.

The inquest into the fire attracted a large crowd of the city's notables and businessmen. Inspector Pender and lawyer Leonard Harper conducted the examination on behalf of the insurance companies. The newspaper reports covered two full pages in small type. Margaret Patterson said she had gone to bed about 11.30 and did not check to see if the fireplaces were dead because Emily Williams had just returned from the theatre with a friend, George Nixon, who left before midnight. William Vigors, clerk of the Supreme Court, had been visiting Mrs Patterson that evening but she said he had left at 10.55. The two women shared the double bed in the back bedroom so there was nobody upstairs. Emily Williams said she had been woken by the sound of breaking glass, and found the room full of smoke. Margaret Patterson then got up and went through to the dining room, where she found the place 'lit up as if from a conflagration', and saw the silhouette of a man in the Cashel Street entrance. (This was probably Sergeant Pratt.) Emily Williams called to her to take some clothes with her so she bundled up a skirt and blouse and they both ran out into the back yard, where they met Sergeant Pratt running along the alleyway.

When Margaret Patterson was closely questioned about the amount of stock she had on the premises, and how she ran her business, it emerged that Emily Williams looked after the bar and gave her the takings at the end of each day. Mrs Patterson said she usually banked the money on a Monday, but had been unwell in recent weeks and a large sum had accumulated. She was extremely vague about her purchases of stock, and said all her accounts had been lost in the fire, but it became apparent that she did not keep regular accounts. Indeed, one of the jurors called attention to the contrast between the precise times Mrs Patterson gave for the departure of William Vigors and the arrival of Emily Williams and George Nixon, and 'her strange forgetfulness of more important matters, such as the money, stock, and business receipts'. The coroner, too, had noted this 'singularity'.

Sergeant Pratt, Albert Bradwell junior, William Harris, Marcus Sandstein and Thomas Brass gave full accounts of the fire. Clerks from various insurance companies provided details of the insurance policies, and John Thompson, accountant at the Bank of Australasia, testified that two days before the fire Mrs Patterson had brought a sealed packet to the bank for safekeeping. She did not say what was in it, and did not make any deposit or fill out a deposit slip. Since the fire she had recovered the package.

The jury retired only briefly, and their foreman, John Ollivier, delivered their decision, that on the morning of 10 March Margaret Patterson and Emily Jane Williams had 'feloniously, wilfully and maliciously set fire to a certain house in the occupation of the said Margaret Patterson with intent ... to defraud certain insurance companies called the Royal and the Australian and Alliance'. The coroner committed them to stand trial at the next session of the Supreme Court.

Margaret Patterson and Emily Williams appeared before Mr Justice Gresson in the Christchurch Supreme Court on 13 June 1870, charged with attempting to defraud the insurance companies and the building's owner, Lawson Cape. Both women pleaded not guilty. They were represented by Thomas Joynt, and Thomas Duncan was the Crown prosecutor. The Canterbury *Police Gazette* described Patterson as a 34-year-old Irish restaurant-keeper, 5ft 6in (167cm) in height, of stout build, with dark hair and brown eyes. Emily Williams was English, aged 20, slightly taller at 169cm, with a pale complexion, brown hair and brown eyes.

Sergeant Pratt described, at length, both the fire and his actions. Then, after some legal niceties were dealt with, the women's depositions were read to the court and questioning of witnesses continued.

William Harris was questioned about Emily Williams's clothing. Sergeant Pratt had denied that she was wearing a cloak, as Albert Bradwell had told the inquest. Harris could not recall whether or not she wore a cloak: 'She appeared to have on a dark dress, and a short jacket ... She had a hat on.'

That ended the first day's proceedings, and the jury spent the night at the Royal Hotel. Next morning Bradwell was questioned closely about the clothing and demeanour of the two women when he saw them in the alleyway. He was sure that Miss Williams wore a long dark cloak, covering her almost from neck to ankle. The two women were frightened and trembling, but 'Miss Williams was more cool than Mrs Patterson'. He was then questioned further about what he saw inside the building and the state of the double bed in the back bedroom. He said the bedclothes looked as if someone had been lying on top of the bed rather than in it.

Harry Feast, police detective, then described his conversations with Mrs Patterson immediately after the fire, in which she had been distraught over the loss of £150 in cash that she said she had in a pocket-book in a drawer in the back bedroom. Feast had gone to investigate the furniture that had been taken out of the burning building but failed to find the pocket-book. Mrs Patterson told him she had lost everything except what she was wearing.

George Nixon then testified that he had walked Emily Williams home after the theatre, and had left her about 11.45pm. On the table was a lighted candle, which she had used to light the gas lamps. There was no fire in the fireplace. He recalled that his companion had been wearing a chignon and hat but took the hat off when they entered the café.

John Thompson from the Bank of Australasia then repeated his evidence about the safe-deposit packet, and Richard Harman, one of the city's most respected businessmen, stated that Mrs Patterson had come to his office to make a declaration before him as a JP about the December fire at the London Restaurant. Joynt objected to this, on the ground that such a declaration was irrelevant to the present case, but Gresson overruled him. A clerk from the agent for the Royal

Insurance Company then gave details of Mrs Patterson's claim for the December fire, and Andrew Duncan, mayor of Christchurch and another highly respected businessman, said he knew Mrs Patterson and produced the declaration she had made to him on 24 March about her December losses.

The Crown prosecutor called further witnesses from the police and fire brigade about the first fire, then called Henry Dodd, the cabman who had taken Mrs Patterson out to Shakespeare's Hotel. So ended the second day of the trial.

The third day started with the fresh evidence of the housemaid, Margaret Regan, which occupied most of the morning. Then Hermann Cohn of Petersen's the jewellers testified that, before the December fire, Mrs Patterson had brought a silver tea service, a gold watch and chain, a locket, a necklace and a gold chain to the shop to be cleaned. However, when she came to pay an account in January and he asked her to take them away she said she had no immediate need of them and would send for them later. He estimated the total value of the items at £25.

Thomas Brass then told the court that he had met Mrs Patterson in the Union Bank the day after the March fire and she had asked him to lend her £20 to employ a solicitor to act for her at the inquest. Brass had replied that he had no money to lend to anyone. She then offered a gold watch and chain as security, and said she had another watch at Petersen's. He told her to ask Petersen's to advance her the money. She said nothing about the fire.

When Thomas Joynt said he would not be calling any witnesses for the defence, the Crown prosecutor, Thomas Duncan, addressed the jury, drawing their attention to the new evidence presented by Margaret Regan, which tended to support the view that the two women had been removing items for safekeeping before the suspicious fire in December 1869. That attempt at insurance fraud had been thwarted by the vigilance of Constable Robert Thompson, who had put out the fire. Duncan suggested that they had made a second and more successful attempt on 10 March. Sergeant Pratt's evidence was crucial to the prosecution case, especially his insistence that he had seen two unconnected fires, one on the stairs and the other on the piano in the café.

The defence's case was that a person's guilt had to be proven beyond reasonable doubt, and there was no evidence to show that the fire had been lit by either Mrs Patterson or Miss Williams. It could have been an accident, perhaps started by a candle left on the sheets of music on top of the piano. Fire Superintendent Harris had told the court that there had been a great many suspicious fires in the central city over the previous year. Joynt invited the jury to believe that the London Restaurant could have been destroyed by a malicious fire-bug.

Mr Justice Gresson's summing-up to the jury was, according to the newspapers, 'lengthy', but none of them reported what he said. The jury retired at 5pm and returned soon after 6pm with a verdict of not guilty. This was a signal for cheers from the packed public gallery, which included many women, until the sheriff, Dr Back, quietened them with a warning that they could be charged with contempt for such unseemly conduct in a court of justice. The two women were discharged, and on leaving the courthouse were greeted with yet more cheers outside.

Little more is known about Margaret Patterson and Emily Williams, except that in January 1875 they presided over two bachelors' tables at a tea meeting held in the Oddfellows' Hall in Lichfield Street, as part of a district meeting of the United Methodist Free Churches, suggesting that they had maintained their place in the church as respectable women. Having been acquitted of arson, Mrs Patterson was able to claim the full amounts of her two insurance policies, which would have more than made up for her alleged loss of cash in the fire.

Though they had been acquitted by a sympathetic jury, the behaviour of the two women must raise some doubts about their innocence. Joynt's refusal to put either in the witness box for cross-examination suggests that he feared they might incriminate themselves. The removal of bags and boxes before the December fire remains questionable, as does Mrs Patterson's deposit of a package for safekeeping at the bank before the March fire, and her leaving valuables for 'cleaning' at the jeweller's. Sergeant Pratt's insistence that he saw two unconnected fires on the premises on 10 March raises the probability that at least one of them had been deliberately lit. The building was secure when he got there, with no signs of a break-in until he himself forced the front door, yet both fires were deep inside the building.

Those of us with suspicious minds may well want to know a lot more about Miss Emily Williams. She had come to live with her friend two years before and helped to run the business after John Patterson died. She had control of the cash coming in. Was she perhaps manipulating an older woman who was not in good health? Was she perhaps taking a small cut of the profits for herself? According to Margaret Patterson the restaurant was not doing well and she had obtained a reduction in her rent. She may have wanted to be rid of the business but she had nowhere else to go unless she could raise the money to rent or buy a house. Knowing that the stock and furniture were well insured, Emily Williams could have planned the arson on her own, trusting that her friend would always give her a home. But why, then, had Margaret Patterson attempted to remove bulky bags and boxes before the December fire? Why had she gone to the trouble of making sworn statements before two pillars of Christchurch society about her losses in both fires? What was in that safe-deposit package? Her behaviour suggests complicity with Emily Williams, but the jury chose to give both women the benefit of the doubt.

The London Restaurant site was on prime commercial land in the middle of the city, and did not remain vacant for long. George Gould offered it to William Pratt, who joined with Thomas Brass to erect a two-storey brick building between Colombo Street and Dunstable House. Pratt had previously acquired the freehold of the latter from David Clarkson. But just before the deal could be completed Pratt suffered a heavy loss in the great Lyttelton fire of 24 October 1870, which gutted the commercial heart of the port town and destroyed his Lyttelton warehouse. According to Gordon

Ogilvie's history of Ballantynes, this seemed to have disheartened him, and no sooner had the new building been completed than he leased Dunstable House to a newcomer, John Ballantyne, and retired from commerce to devote himself to his church and local body politics. Ballantynes went on to become a Canterbury institution and the city's oldest surviving department store, rebuilt after a tragic fire in 1949 to survive even the major earthquakes of 2010 and 2011.[1]

The London Restaurant case was also the making of one of nineteenth-century Canterbury's most prominent lawyers. Thomas Ingham Joynt had come to New Zealand from Ireland in 1856 on the recommendation of his Dublin friend, Henry Barnes Gresson. He was clerk of the Magistrate's Court in Lyttelton until 1858, when he was articled to the Crown prosecutor, Thomas Duncan. Joynt went out on his own account in 1863, living in a little three-room cottage in Lichfield Street while he built up his practice as a criminal pleader. His wide reading and exceptional facility with words also made him popular as a drafter of legal documents in clear, concise language. His defence of Margaret Patterson and Emily Williams was later described as 'brilliant', and after his success with this case his legal practice rapidly increased. Joynt was also the Kaiapoi representative in the Canterbury Provincial Council and provincial solicitor under the Rolleston administration until the abolition of the provinces in 1876. When he died in 1907 he was New Zealand's senior King's Counsel.[2]

CHAPTER ELEVEN

PERSISTENT OFFENDERS

A SUBURBAN DELIGHT.
Dark Party (with a
ticket-of-leave, of
course) – 'Ax yer
pardon, sir! But if you
was agoing down this
dark lane, p'raps you'd
allow me and this here
young man to go along
with yer, 'cos, yer see,
there aint no perlice
about, and we're so
precious feared o'
being garrotted!'

John Leech, *Four Hundred
Humorous Illustrations*,
2nd edn. 1862

Some names stand out from the court reports and the *Police
Gazette* as repeat offenders who were so often in trouble with
the police that they became familiar faces in the Magistrate's Court.
We have already noticed a few of them, such as the prostitute Emma
Craigie, who by the 1870s was being described as 'an old offender'.
In fact most of the recidivists were women, and most of them were
prostitutes. But there were a few notorious men as well, such as
William Crawley, alias 'Cockney Bill', or James Clark, alias 'The
Brusher'. We shall first investigate the latter's career before return-
ing to the loose and rowdy women of Christchurch.

James Clark was a former convict who had come to New Zealand in 1865 from Australia, where he had acquired his nickname over the previous decade or so. In Australian slang a 'brusher' is someone who departs, leaving debts unpaid. He had, as it were, given his creditors the brush-off. He first tried his luck on the Otago goldfields, but was sentenced repeatedly for robbery and vagrancy before moving to Canterbury in 1866. He then received several sentences in South Canterbury, one of which was six months with hard labour for robbing a drunken man at Temuka, before he moved to Christchurch.

In a Charles Dickens novel 'The Brusher' would have figured as a 'bruiser', the sort of Bill Sykes character who was often drunk and quick to use his fists. In February 1869 he appeared in the Magistrate's Court on a charge of being found drunk and incapable. He admitted the offence but said he would reform if let off. Magistrate Bowen noted that he had nine previous convictions, and that this was too long a list to merit leniency, so he was fined 40s, or 48 hours in prison if he could not come up with the money. He was back in court in September for being drunk and riotous in a licensed house and was fined 10s, but there were probably other similar offences in between that were not noticed by the newspapers.

Bowen's patience had evidently run out when Clark appeared again in March 1870 on yet another drunk and disorderly charge. The magistrate said he had been living a drunken loafing life ever since he had been in the province, and was evidently incorrigible, so he would go to prison and make himself useful for the next three months doing some hard labour. In Canterbury that meant the hard labour gang at the Lyttelton Gaol, who helped to build the stone retaining walls that can still be seen supporting the port town's steep streets, though some fell down in the earthquakes of 2010 and 2011.

The Canterbury *Police Gazette* described Clark as an Irishman, occupation labourer (which might have been true, at least for the next three months), age 35, 5ft 7in (169cm) tall, of stout build and pale complexion, with light brown hair and grey eyes. In the column for remarks it was noted that he was scarred over both eyes, and that he had a flat nose with 'coarse and flabby features'.

Clark was no sooner out of prison in April 1871 than he was in trouble again, this time on a much more serious charge, that of being a rogue and a vagabond and resisting a constable while in the discharge of his duty. Constable Eares, who sported 'a severe black eye', told the court he had seen Clark in the Criterion Hotel at 10 o'clock the previous evening, trying to make a drunken man fight with him. 'There was considerable noise, and a crowd of from twenty to thirty persons was collected round the door. After a short time the drunken man went away, and [Clark] followed him, calling him very disgraceful names.' Eares, watching from down the street, saw Clark pull the drunken man into a right-of-way between the *Lyttelton Times* office and the Central Hotel. From 'previous knowledge of the prisoner' the constable was sure that Clark was intent on robbery so went up and took him into custody, whereupon Clark 'struck him a severe blow in the eye, and became very violent, kicking and biting ... in a furious manner'. Eares was forced to use his baton to protect himself and needed the assistance of two men before he could subdue Clark.

In court, Clark's forehead 'bore strong evidence of rough work, the right temple being covered with blood'. Sergeant O'Connor told the court he had known Clark for 12 or 14 years, part of the time in Australia, and knew him to be 'a most dangerous character'. He was a vagrant who made his living by robbing drunken men, usually by picking a fight with them in a pub. Sergeant McKnight then produced several pages of police records detailing Clark's previous offences in Otago and South Canterbury. He had accumulated 20 convictions since 1866, including fines for drunkenness totalling £13, and the amount of time he had spent in prison came to only a few days short of three years. It would be better for the public, said the magistrate, if Clark had a longer term in gaol: he sentenced him to two years with hard labour.

He was out of prison again in 1873, but had not changed his former ways and was picked up in May that year by Constable Kennedy for being drunk and disorderly. Noting that it was his first offence since coming out of prison, Bowen dismissed him with a caution, but Clark was back in court that August, this time charged with having been drunk and disorderly, using obscene language in a public place and assaulting the police while in the execution of their duty. This time he got a month in prison with hard labour.

In February 1874 he was in court again on the same set of charges, and in view of his many previous convictions Bowen sent him down for six months with hard labour. He was released in July 1874 but was immediately in trouble again, for causing a disturbance at the Golden Fleece Hotel on the corner of Armagh and Colombo streets. The barman at the hotel described how Clark came into the bar 'under the influence of liquor, and, after talking a great deal about being a pugilist, and having fought several battles, took off his coat and wanted a fight'. The barman refused to serve him and ordered him to leave, 'whereupon he used very offensive language'. Since Clark refused to go away, the proprietor, George Oram, 'gave him into custody'. Clark told the court that 'he did not think he had done what was imputed to him, but said, if he had, he humbly begged pardon, and hoped the Bench would deal leniently with him, when he would not offend again'. He then 'asserted that he was not intoxicated' and called on Constable Emson, who had arrested him, to prove it. Emson said Clark had been 'under the influence of liquor, but could not be called drunk'.

Magistrate Bowen observed that Clark had been out of gaol only a few days and had already been twice before the court. The accused had apparently done nothing but 'wander from bar to bar, and made himself a perfect terror to all the people he came across'. In the past eight years he had spent no less than five years and four months in gaol, and had contrived to get 28 convictions recorded against him. Clark said that if he was dealt with leniently this time, he would 'most positively reform', but Bowen pointed out that he had made this same promise 27 times out of the 28 he had been in court. Having just served time in prison on a vagrancy charge he would not be dealt with as a vagrant, but under the Public House Ordinance, and the full penalty would be imposed. He would be fined £5 and serve 14 days in prison, and if the fine was not paid he would spend another month in prison, with hard labour.

Some people never learn, but perhaps we should not expect too much of a hardened alcoholic. In March 1875 'The Brusher' repeated the same offence at the Market Hotel, just a few steps up Colombo Street from the Golden Fleece. Constable Watt and the proprietor of the Market, Henry Haddrill, gave evidence that Clark had been refused drink and became 'very riotous', and that when the constable arrived to arrest him he had 'used great violence, tearing the constable's trowsers [*sic*] and assaulting him in a most determined manner'. Inspector Buckley told the court that Clark had been only a fortnight out of gaol. Clark repeated his usual promise to reform. Magistrate G. L. Mellish from Picton, who was relieving Bowen for his annual holiday, fined him £5 and ordered him to pay for the damage to the constable's trousers. If he could not pay, he would go back to prison for a week with hard labour.

By September 1875 Clark had accumulated 33 convictions, and when he appeared yet again on a charge of drunkenness and obscene language he was dismissed with a caution after promising to clear out of Canterbury at once. As he left the court Clark thanked the magistrate profusely, 'earnestly invoking blessings on his Worship, for the leniency shown him'. This time he kept his word, and there is no further mention of this James Clark in the newspapers. He probably went back to Australia.

This must have been a great relief to the other James Clark in Christchurch, a respectable boot-maker and saddler who lived in Salisbury Street and was a member of the Masonic Lodge. His wife died suddenly in February 1875 and he moved to Peterborough Street. He may have fallen into bad company, for in April 1886 a woman named Mary Ryan was found dead in his house, having suffered a stroke from excessive drinking.

In *A Woman of Good Character: Single women as immigrant settlers in nineteenth-century New Zealand* Charlotte Macdonald describes Eliza Lambert as 'the most infamous' of the assisted migrants who turned to prostitution after their arrival in Canterbury, but Emma Craigie would come a very close second for that dubious distinction.

Eliza Lambert was only 14 when she was selected by James Edward FitzGerald from an industrial school in Surrey for the chance of a better life in the colonies. She came out on the first voyage of the *Mystery*, arriving in March 1859 along with her friend Emma Bennett. On the voyage she stole beer and gin from the ship's stores and drank with the crew in their quarters, very likely granting them various favours besides. She was often in trouble with the law in the 1860s, as we have seen, but on 7 June 1869 she was in court on a much more serious charge: stabbing a man in a brothel. The victim, Edward McCormack, was still recovering when the case was heard before Magistrate Bowen and his remarkable statement, made on 7 May, the morning after the incident, was read to the court:

> Last night, at eleven o'clock, I was ... on the other side of the railway [in Sydenham], in the direction of the Prince of Wales Hotel. I was in company with a young woman ... I think they call her Eliza. She is stout and has a full face. I had been drinking with her, but I do not know where, for I am a stranger in the town. I only came in on Sunday night. The knife produced belongs to me. When I awoke this morning it was under the bed, and was covered with blood. I had not got the wound when I went to bed. There was another man in the house when I went to bed, but I do not know who he was. I went to bed with the girl I have described. She said in the morning she thought it must have been her who did it, and asked me to forgive her. I came away from the house after that. She said she was sorry. I had been with the girl since Sunday or Monday, but I am not sure which.

McCormack had had £23 on him when he left the West Coast and came through Browning Pass; by the time he talked to the police he thought only about 18d was left.

There was some drinking going on before we went to bed, but I do not know whether I had any. Another man and woman stayed in the house all night, but I did not see them. I believe the girl I slept with was the person from whom I received the wound. When I had some conversation with the girl she told me that I dared her to do it, and I ought not to have done so. I asked her for the knife, and she said it was under the bed. She picked up the knife from under the bed and gave it to me. I saw that it was covered with blood … When I showed her the blood on the knife, she said she was sorry, but said I had dared her to do it. I accused her of having done it …

The Saturday before the hearing McCormack had confirmed his account and added, 'I don't recollect whether there was a quarrel or not. I don't recollect anything until the next morning.'

Dr Prins, who treated McCormack at the hospital, found a puncture wound on the left side of his chest. The whole of his left side was 'much swollen' and he was having great difficulty breathing. His lung had probably been penetrated and he took a long while to recover. He was very lucky to be alive.

Eliza Lambert was also very lucky that he was still alive, otherwise she might have been facing a charge of murder. Sharing the house with her in Colombo Street, Sydenham, was Ann Bowdy, who told the court that McCormack had stayed about four days with Eliza Lambert, going out with her to drink in various public houses and returning by cab. They started on amicable terms but often came back drunk and quarrelling. On the night in question they were 'wrangling a bit' and had some sharp words.

According to Detective Harry Feast, when he arrested Lambert she said McCormack had called her an offensive name and she had told him that if she had a knife she would run him through. He then dared her to do so, and gave her his clasp knife. She took it and threw it at him. He was sitting on the bed at the time and it struck him in the left of his chest. He afterwards slept with her through the night. In the morning she saw some drops of blood on the floor but there was no blood in the bed.

Eliza Lambert declined to make any statement in her defence, or call witnesses, and she was committed for trial at the next session of the Supreme Court. As she left the court she 'slammed the door in a very violent and passionate manner'. On 2 September 1869 her case came before the Supreme Court, where she was found guilty of wilfully stabbing and wounding and was sentenced to a year in prison with hard labour. She had no sooner come out of gaol than she was arrested, with her fellow prostitute Jane Crawford, on a charge of being drunk and disorderly, and went back inside for 48 hours.

Then in December she appeared in the Magistrate's Court with Minnie Thompson, Margaret Clarke, Flora Martin, James Ryan and Duncan Cameron, charged with being the owners and frequenters of a disorderly brothel in Lichfield Street East. The *Lyttelton Times* reporter described them as 'a dirty depraved-looking lot'. Inspector Pender said that when he went to the house there was every appearance of a fight having taken place, with broken bottles in a shed and blood spattered on various items in the house. The occupants were all in a state of drunkenness. Cameron had a cut over his eye, while Thompson and Martin were 'semi-nude'. The house had been very disorderly for some time and neighbours had made many complaints. When Clarke and Lambert insisted they had only been visiting the house that night and were not responsible for the previous disturbances, Magistrate Bowen gave them the benefit of the doubt and dismissed them with a stern warning. The others each got three months in prison.

Apart from a three-month sentence for indecent conduct in a public thoroughfare later that month, Eliza Lambert kept out of trouble until she faced a similar charge in January 1873, and thereafter her name disappears from the Christchurch newspapers.

Emma Craigie's story is equally colourful, as we have seen in previous chapters, but hers had a sad ending. By the time she was arrested for drunkenness at the Criterion Hotel in October 1868 she had

14 previous convictions, so Bowen sentenced her to two months in prison with hard labour. Her cheeky exchange with the magistrate in November that year, after being convicted for being drunk and disorderly and exposing herself in a public place, had an unexpected result: the police then charged her with being of unsound mind. Bowen consulted the coroner, Dr Coward, and he in turn consulted Dr Powell, who agreed that her behaviour was becoming increasingly bizarre. Bowen said he would write to the colonial secretary to ask if there were sufficient grounds to have her removed to the lunatic asylum, but the reply was apparently in the negative.

This episode must have given her a fright since she kept out of trouble for nearly a year. When she appeared before the magistrate in August 1869, Bowen said he was 'always gratified to notice any apparent improvement, however slight', and would deal leniently with her. She was dismissed with a warning. His leniency may be explained by his realisation that she was now a hopeless alcoholic and at risk of an early death.

In 1869, when she was 36, the Canterbury *Police Gazette* described Emma Craigie as a short woman of medium build, only 5ft 2in tall (157cm), with a pale complexion, dark hair and blue eyes. She had two tattoos – a cross on her left arm and a heart on the back of her right hand. Her two children, of unknown paternity, were in state care at the orphanage.

One of her favourite haunts was the theatre, where her extrovert behaviour in the audience was more likely to be tolerated if the performance warranted criticism. But sometimes she overstepped the mark, and in September 1869 she spent a week in prison with hard labour after being ejected from the theatre for drunkenness and obscene language. The *Lyttelton Times* called her 'A Public Nuisance', one of the city's oldest female offenders, and apparently 'an incorrigible'. Later that same month she was sentenced to two months in gaol for wilful damage to private property (unspecified), and in November she broke a large window at the Warwick Hotel while being drunk and disorderly. Bowen remarked that her behaviour had been 'more than usually disgraceful', but he fined her only 20s and costs.

Craigie managed to stay out of trouble for all of 1870, and when arrested in February 1871 for disorderly conduct at the theatre she was let off with a caution in view of her improved behaviour. But the very next month she was involved in a noisy drunken brawl at a brothel, in the course of which she had both her eyes 'severely blackened'. She and Mary Holmes were each sentenced to one week's prison with hard labour.

On St Patrick's Day 1871 she was arrested at the police depot for being drunk and noisy. Her only excuse was that she had called 'to see how all were getting on'. Some might say this suggests she was a good-hearted whore, but she was drunk and disorderly several more times during that year, amassing a grand total of 27 convictions, rather more than Eliza Lambert.

The *Police Gazette* now described her build as 'slight' rather than stout, suggesting that her alcoholism had been affecting her appetite and her health. She even appeared as a police witness about this time, to testify that a publican had sold her a bottle of port wine after closing hours at Barrett's Hotel. Then, to everyone's surprise, there was a brief notice in the *Lyttelton Times* in September 1871 announcing that she had been married, by Dean Henry Jacobs himself, no less, to one Frederick Palmer, whose name, unlike hers, does not appear in the court reports or the *Police Gazette* of this period. Whoever he was, he was a brave man to take such a notorious woman as his wife. Or perhaps he was more adept at avoiding the police.

Only three months later Emma Palmer, as she now was, was arrested, along with Jane Crawford, Fanny Harding, Ellen Thompson and Helena Stone, on a charge of keeping a disorderly house. Constable Wilson, responding to a complaint, had gone to the address at midnight on Saturday and found the place 'full of cabmen and seamen, numbering about 20 ... There was a great disturbance going on, and noise created by dancing and singing.' Angry neighbours were out in the street, unable to sleep and threatening to take matters into their own hands. One man said he had had to keep his children indoors, 'on account of the bad language used by the children of the accused'.

Strangely enough, Magistrate Bowen dismissed the charges, using the impeccable logic that a disorderly house no longer existed at that address. Ellen Thompson had in fact been in prison on the night in question. But he asked the police to be sure to report any cabmen they found making disturbances in brothels, as their licences could then be revoked. Inspector Pender remarked that although the rowdy women had all left that address, 'the disturbances would be as great wherever they lived'.

Once again, Emma Palmer kept out of the Christchurch courts for a year, during 1872, but that was because she and her husband had gone to make a fresh start in Wellington, until the police there ordered her to leave their province. She returned to Christchurch in January 1873, only to take up to her old ways and be locked up for three months with hard labour for vagrancy, which was the contemporary euphemism for prostitution. By now she had 32 convictions, which must be something of a record for a woman in Canterbury at that time. Her convictions were now almost all for obscene language while being drunk and disorderly in a public place. She sadly fitted the newspaper's label of 'a public nuisance'. Finally, in March 1874, Dr Powell and Dr Patrick Doyle committed her to the Sunnyside Lunatic Asylum in Lincoln Road as a person of unsound mind, where she died in 1876, aged 43.

Combing through the surviving volumes of the Canterbury *Police Gazette* from 1868 to 1871 one cannot help being struck by the predominance of vagrancy and 'drunk and disorderly' convictions among the women listed. Male offenders committed a much wider range of offences, with larceny, assault, forgery, malicious damage to property, housebreaking, fighting in the street and simple drunkenness among the most common. (Men were also more likely to be charged with indecent exposure, from their widespread habit of urinating in alleyways.) Another strong impression arising from the pages of the *Gazette* is that, like many women in that age of poorer nutrition, most of Christchurch's prostitutes in the 1860s were short: their heights are mostly between 5ft (152cm) and 5ft 4in (162cm), with a few even shorter. Their build is most commonly given as 'stout'. One of the shortest was Mary Jane Huckley, at 4ft 10in (146cm). Contrary to a widely believed myth, not all were Irish. Of the 25 prostitutes given prison sentences in Christchurch between 1868 and 1871, 10 were from England, 10 were from Scotland and only five were from Ireland.

Thanks to a diligent police constable, who included detailed personal descriptions for a few months in 1870, we even know what they wore when discharged from prison. Straw hats with a feather or ribbon, and elastic-sided boots, were standard. Mary Ann Robinson sported a black silk jacket and lavender silk dress, with a blue veil, as well as a black straw hat and elastic-sided boots. (In February 1871 she was also lame, from an ulcerated leg.) Unlike male offenders, who often had tattoos as distinguishing marks, prostitutes usually had none; Emma Craigie's tattoos were the exception rather than the rule. The women were more likely to be identified by scars: Margaret Bowen's face was marked by smallpox, Jane Glass had a scar near her right eye, Annie Driscoll had a scar on her right wrist, Ellen Talbot had a scar on her left cheek, as did Jane Ballinger. One of the men, James McDonald, a former convict from New South Wales, had a face badly disfigured by disease, probably syphilis, as his nose was 'gone'. One of the most curious personal descriptions was that of a 52-year-old 'well-known thief' and housebreaker named Walter Johnson: 'Smooth face, little or no beard or whiskers, left eye usually closed, no front upper teeth, long thin face, pale complexion, and a supercilious grin when talking.' Such a description would surely make him instantly recognisable anywhere.

Public concern about the increase in prostitution in Christchurch in the 1860s, commonly blamed on the arrival of single migrant women, led to a town hall meeting on 22 November 1867 chaired by Dean Jacobs and attended by Judge Henry Gresson, Magistrate Christopher Bowen, members of parliament and numerous clergy. There were no women present. The men were mainly concerned that the prostitutes were becoming too bold and brazen, conducting their profession quite openly. A clear majority favoured some system of state regulation and medical inspection. Superintendent William Rolleston took the meeting's concerns to the central government in Wellington, where a select committee was set up to draft a bill. In fact they drafted two, the Contagious Diseases Bill and the Vagrant Amendment Bill, both of which were introduced by Rolleston and passed into law in August 1869. What the newspapers called 'the New Vagrant Bill' made it an offence for any prostitute to loiter in the streets and public thoroughfares, or for any hotel proprietor to allow prostitutes to gather on his premises. It was even illegal for any person to sing an obscene song in a public place. It was left to the police to decide who was or was not a 'common prostitute'. The onus was on the woman to prove that she was not a prostitute. With these new powers the Christchurch police cracked down hard on the ladies of the night early in 1870, and Magistrate Bowen, kind-hearted as he was, sent them to prison for periods ranging from a week to three months. But most of them were soon out again, and there had to be a second crackdown in October, when a dozen prostitutes were again sent to prison.

Sometimes linkages can be made between juvenile criminals and their parents. The seven-year-old John Darby released from prison in December 1868, after serving seven days and enduring a whipping for stealing, was almost certainly the son of the prostitute Elizabeth Darby, who was twice charged with keeping a house of ill fame, and had a string of convictions for vagrancy in this period. The 11-year-old William Pepperell who was given the same sentence in April 1871 for stealing fruit was almost certainly the son of Thomas Pepperell, who had shot a man accidentally at Craigieburn Station in 1868, and spent a month in prison in 1869 for helping himself from the till at the Criterion Hotel.

We cannot choose our parents, and even at this distance in time it is hard not to feel sorry for the children of people such as Emma Craigie. In such a censorious society as Christchurch in the nineteenth century they were burdened with heavy handicaps long before they reached adulthood. Yet for all those who followed their parents into a life of crime there were many more who resolved to keep on the right side of the law rather than repeat the mistakes and miseries of their parents.

CHAPTER TWELVE

THE CAMBRIDGE TERRACE MURDER OF 1871

Christchurch Supreme Court, designed by Alexander Lean, built 1869–74 and demolished in 1980 after years of neglect. This was one of Christchurch's most significant public buildings, dominating the vista of Victoria Square, yet it was allowed to decay while plans for a modern court building were long delayed.

Brittenden collection

Though it was a straightforward case in which the verdict was never in any doubt, the Cambridge Terrace murder of 1871 is one of nineteenth-century New Zealand's best-known homicides, partly because it involved a wealthy landowner, and partly because of the legend that later became attached to the victim's gravestone. Until recently, however, it has been known as 'the Park Terrace murder', owing to some confusion as to the exact location of the house in which the murder took place. Sergeant McKnight initially told the papers that the house was on the corner of Cambridge Terrace (then known as Canterbury Terrace) and Salisbury Street, leading later writers to assume it was on Park Terrace, but the house owned by Sir Frederick Weld and rented by William Robinson was on the corner of Cambridge Terrace and Montreal Street, close by Dr Coward's house and the hospital.

There are numerous accounts in print of this murder, ranging from the revisionist argument of Charles A. L. Treadwell in his *Notable New Zealand Trials* and the brief summary in David Gee's *The Devil's Own Brigade* to Sherwood Young's *Guilty on the Gallows: Famous capital crimes of New Zealand*. A television documentary-drama about the case, written by Isa Moynihan and starring George Henare, screened as long ago as 1976, and several versions of the trial are available online from various amateur websites, all copied from previous printed accounts. The most detailed reconstruction is that by Margaret Wigley, in her biography of her great-grandfather, *'Ready Money': The life of William Robinson*. However, none of these accounts mentions what happened in the Market Place in Christchurch immediately after the trial, which was almost as sensational as the trial itself.

The *Star* greeted its readers on 10 January 1871 with the rare headline 'Horrible Tragedy', and in its best journalistic style informed them that:

> An occurrence unequalled in our provincial annals, and fitted to be classed amongst the worst deeds of personal violence, startled the city from its wonted equanimity yesterday afternoon. The details were at first received, even by the most credulous, with complete disbelief, but enquiry unfortunately showed that horrible as they were, they were but too true. The tragedy comprises the death of one female and the almost miraculous escape of another – all being the act of one man, their fellow-servant's violence.

This is what appeared to have happened. On 9 January a black

South American butler named Simon Cedeno, aged 28, had attacked two Irish housemaids at a house rented by the wealthy Canterbury runholder William 'Ready Money' Robinson. He had wounded Catherine Glynn (the newspapers at first thought it was another servant, Bridget Murray), then pursued Margaret ('Maggie') Burke to the dining room, where he stabbed her several times with a sharp breadknife in front of Mrs Robinson, before he was overpowered by a visitor, Patrick Campbell. Margaret Burke from Galway, aged just 22, died from a stab wound to the heart.

Cedeno was brought before magistrate Christopher Bowen the next day. A large crowd had gathered outside, while inside the courtroom was 'crowded to suffocation' by a throng of curious onlookers. Cedeno was described by a reporter as 'tall and of slight build', with 'a stubborn lowering look on his features', but 'appeared quite steady and free from nervousness'. Another reporter noted that he was not as black as a pure-bred Negro or African, but had a lighter coffee-coloured complexion and long hair, indicating that he was of mixed-race origins. He came from Bogota, in the highlands of Colombia, South America, and had been working at a hotel in Panama when William Robinson and his family were returning from a trip to England some four years earlier. The proprietor said he had also worked in Havana, Cuba, and gave him a good reference. On the strength of this, Robinson hired him as a butler and brought him to New Zealand, where he proved an excellent servant at the mansion on Robinson's North Canterbury run, Cheviot Hills, and at his Christchurch townhouse on Cambridge Terrace, rented from the Weld family.

Sergeant McKnight told the court that he was on duty at the police depot about 4pm the previous afternoon when Cedeno was brought there by Campbell and a groom named John Price. They told him that Cedeno had stabbed two of the servant girls and one of them was dead. After locking Cedeno in a cell, Sergeant McKnight went to the Robinson house and there found Maggie Burke, 'quite dead, and lying in a large pool of blood'. Campbell had produced the knife, its blade and part of the handle covered in blood. McKnight returned to the police depot and told Cedeno that he would be charged with murdering Margaret Burke. Cedeno immediately asked, 'Is she quite dead?' Before McKnight could caution him, he went on to say, 'They have all been murdering me up there. Ready-money Robinson has been nearly killing me.' Then he suddenly stopped and said no more. Cedeno spoke English, but 'very imperfectly'. He declined to answer any questions. In view of the inquest to be held that afternoon, Bowen remanded Cedeno in custody until the following morning. As Cedeno left the court, the crowd greeted him with groans and hisses.

The inquest was held at the Royal Hotel in Oxford Terrace, just across the river from the crime scene and the nearest available venue to the hospital morgue. John Ollivier was elected foreman of the inquest jury, which included such Christchurch notables as F. A. Bishop, Frederick Hobbs, miller William Derisley Wood and George Gould. After viewing the body the jury assembled at the hotel, with a large contingent of the press and members of the public in attendance. Cedeno, standing handcuffed, was asked if he wanted an interpreter, and he replied that although he understood English very well he wished to have one. George Conrad Fownes was sworn in that capacity. As the evidence was given, he conveyed it to Cedeno in Spanish.

McKnight repeated the evidence he had already given at the Magistrate's Court, and Patrick Campbell then gave his account of events as an eye-witness. He had been in the hall when Maggie Burke rushed past, pursued by Cedeno, who was calling out, 'Do you speak of my girl? You call my girl Mary!' Campbell followed them into the dining room, where Eliza Robinson and her five daughters were taking tea. He had not seen the knife in Cedeno's hand when he was in the hall but now he saw it, and grabbed Cedeno's right arm, while seizing him around the neck with his left arm. Maggie was screaming, and stumbled and fell over a dining chair. Cedeno fell on her and Campbell fell on him. Cedeno raised her left arm and plunged the knife repeatedly into her side, with such force that part of the handle also entered her body. Campbell managed to stop some of the blows, and shouted, 'You will kill her, you brute!' Cedeno had looked up and said, 'Yes, I will kill.' He continued to struggle and inflict more wounds. His rage seemed uncontrollable.

Eliza Robinson had the presence of mind to hustle her daughters out of the room and tell them to fetch the groom. She then stepped forward and tried to take the knife from Cedeno, getting a cut on her finger. In a calm, authoritative voice she then said, 'Give me the knife, Cedeno.' Campbell had pulled him off the girl, and Cedeno at once handed it over, saying, 'I give it to you, Ma'am.' Maggie Burke got up, taking two or three steps before she collapsed on the hearth-rug, bleeding profusely. Price then came in and helped Campbell to restrain Cedeno, who by now was quite calm. Mrs Robinson said, 'Take him away,' and Cedeno said, 'Yes, take me to the police.'

The other servant, Catherine Glynn, had fled upstairs to her bedroom, where the Robinson daughters found her and staunched the bleeding from her neck wounds. Dr Henry Prins soon arrived and attended to her, after confirming that Maggie Burke was dead. Prins gave his medical evidence to the inquest, and the coroner, Dr Coward, remarked that the evidence seemed conclusive.

When asked if he would like to employ a solicitor Cedeno declined, saying it would be of no use at all. The seriousness of his position was again explained to him but he still declined. A reporter noted that he 'conversed freely, standing all the time, and was apparently not at all dismayed by his position'. In his account of the inquest the same reporter had noticed that, just as Dr Prins started to give his evidence, Mrs Robinson rose to leave the courtroom, and Cedeno had politely called out to her, 'Goodbye, Ma'am.'

Next morning Cedeno was back in the Magistrate's Court for the rest of his adjourned hearing. This time the crowd was even larger, some people having waited since an hour before the regular opening time. The courtroom was again 'speedily crowded almost to suffocation', and some people stood on the windowsills outside to catch a glimpse of the prisoner. Groom John Price now added a few more details. He had worked as a cowboy in Mexico, and could understand some of the mixture of Spanish and English that had fallen from Cedeno's lips. He said that in the cab on the way to the police depot Cedeno had talked excitedly, and at one point said, 'Yes, I kill two [girls]. That's nothing in my country. People call me wild man, mad man, but I am not.'

After being cautioned, Cedeno then made the following statement:

> Mr. Robinson brought me to this country four years and four months ago. I was a very good servant to Mr. Robinson at the Cheviot Hills Station. Mr Robinson gave me a scolding. He said, 'Black nigger, black heart;' and I said to him, 'Mr Robinson, give me my accounts, because I do not wish to stay,' and he said, 'Very well, if you want your accounts I will charge you with all your clothes.' I said, 'Very well; give me my right money.' That is about fourteen months ago, and if he had given me my money then what occurred on Monday at four o'clock would not have taken place. Mrs. Robinson was very kind to me, but Mr. Robinson was not. When there was a dinner party, Mr. Robinson, in the presence of his visitors, molested me by telling them in my presence that I had a black heart. That is my statement, and I am now resigned to what the law may do with me.

The jury did not even retire, but agreed unanimously on a verdict of wilful murder. Cedeno was committed to stand trial at the next session of the Supreme Court.

After Cedeno was formally committed, Inspector Pender drew the magistrate's attention to the behaviour of the crowd, and asked him to warn them that it should not be repeated. Bowen then pointed out to the public gallery that the prisoner was not yet condemned and 'no demonstrations should be made against him'. The crowd in the courtroom remained silent, but as Cedeno was being taken away in a horse-drawn cab the crowd outside again 'hooted him loudly'.

While waiting for the Supreme Court session set down for March 1871, the newspapers did their best to find out all they could about Cedeno and the two servants he had attacked. They described him as 28 years of age, about 5ft 8in in height (172cm), of slight build, 'and for a man of colour ... good-looking'. In conversations through an interpreter he was 'very excitable', but gave 'great proof of intelligence': 'altogether he is of a superior stamp to the ordinary run of coloured men'. Cedeno was a Catholic and engaged to be married. The wedding arrangements had all been made, but he had been 'chaffed' about it several times by the female servants at the Robinson house, who had allegedly taunted him by saying such things as, 'Why would a white girl want to marry a nigger like you?' The relatives of Maggie Burke and Catherine Glynn, who were cousins, had warned them to stop taunting him, and so had their Catholic priest, Father Jean Claude Chervier, just the weekend before the attacks. In response to these warnings the two women had avoided speaking to Cedeno at all on the Monday, and their silence may have fuelled his rage.

Maggie Burke was buried in the Catholic section of the Barbadoes Street Cemetery on 11 January, with Father Chervier conducting the service. There was great sympathy for her from the general public and Christchurch's large Irish community, with an estimated 500 people attending the funeral.

All this while William Robinson had been travelling north to Cheviot, taking a prize bull to his station. Cedeno is alleged to have said on his way to the police depot that it was lucky Robinson was busy with the bull, otherwise he would have killed his master too. A telegram was sent to Cheviot Hills with news of the murder, and a shepherd was dispatched on horseback to find Robinson en route. He at once turned back for Christchurch, leaving the bull in the care of two stationhands.

The Supreme Court trial of Cedeno for the murder of Maggie Burke opened on 8 March before Mr Justice Gresson. The registrar read out the indictment, which is worth quoting as an example of the legal language of the day:

> Prisoner, you stand indicted by the name of Simon Cedeno that, not having the fear of God before your eyes, but being moved and seduced by the instigation of the Devil, on the 9th day of

January, in the year of our Lord one thousand eight hundred and seventy-one, you feloniously and wilfully, and of your malice aforethought, did kill and murder Margaret Burke, against the peace of our Lady the Queen, her Crown and dignity. How say you? Are you guilty or not guilty of the felony with which you stand indicted?

The indictment was translated into Spanish by Fownes, and Cedeno replied, 'Not guilty.' Thomas Duncan was the Crown prosecutor, and Thomas Joynt had been appointed for the defence. As the jurors were called, four were challenged by the prisoner and 12 were ordered to stand aside by the Crown. The registrar announced that the panel had been exhausted. Gresson said that as Duncan had not yet challenged peremptorily, the names of those ordered to stand aside should be replaced in the box and balloted for. The first name chosen was not challenged, and he completed the required number.

The prosecution called the same witnesses as in the lower court hearing, with two additions: chimneysweep James O'Brien, who had visited the house just before the murder, and had seen Cedeno in the scullery with a glass in one hand and a knife in the other; and Catherine Glynn, the survivor of Cedeno's frenzied attack. She was attended by a nurse, and allowed to give her evidence while seated. Very nervous, and with her face and neck badly disfigured, she burst into tears several times. Catherine Glynn told the court that while Maggie Burke had been scrubbing in the kitchen, Cedeno was looking at her 'in the most awful manner'. He had not performed any of his usual tasks that day and was just sitting brooding in the butler's pantry. Catherine Glynn was emptying some water into the sink and humming to herself when Cedeno grabbed her from behind, pulling her head back by her hair, saying, 'I have caught you now.' At first too frightened to speak, she cried, 'O merciful Jesus' as he raised the knife he was holding and cut her face and neck. As she fell against the pump she heard him say, 'You're done for.' She then fainted, and when she came around there was nobody there. She ran around to the front of the house and through a side window saw

Maggie Burke stumbling over chairs in the dining room. Through the front window she next saw her cousin lying on the hearth-rug and Cedeno being held by Patrick Campbell. She had then retreated upstairs to her own room.

When asked if there had been any friction between Cedeno and the other servants, Glynn said he had behaved kindly towards them, though he was sometimes very surly, and was not in the habit of helping them with their work. Here Cedeno interrupted and said, 'I used to help them.' She then admitted that he was 'obliging, and did little things for us'. A few months before the murder she had seen him quarrel with Maggie Burke, and he had struck the table with his fist and threatened to beat her, but she had warned him that he would 'catch it' if he dared to touch her. After that they seemed to get on with no further ill-feeling. Catherine Glynn also recalled one evening when Cedeno seemed to be in a terrible rage. He was pumping water with such vigour that they feared he would break the pump. He did not use any threatening words or gestures towards the girls, but they were frightened by his anger and went upstairs. On the day of the murder she had noticed something so strange in his manner that it drew her attention. He sat staring at Maggie, then 'repeatedly looking up towards the sky'. Before that day she had never seen Cedeno raise a hand to any of his fellow servants.

Dr Prins was the last witness, to repeat the medical evidence, and that concluded the case for the Crown. Joynt said he had no witnesses to call. Interestingly, Cedeno's sworn statement at the inquest was not read out. The Crown prosecutor summarised the facts of the case and concluded that it was a matter of wilful and premeditated murder. Cedeno was not fit to live in society, and ought to be punished by death, as an example to others who may be tempted to commit a similar crime. Astonishingly, as he sat down, the public gallery broke into applause, until the registrar called for silence in court.

In his address for the defence, Joynt referred to the community's deep-seated desire for revenge over the death of an innocent young woman, and said some people had told him he was wrong to attempt any defence of this man. He urged the jury to divest themselves of all prejudice. Unthinking and institutionalised racism is not a new phenomenon, and had its part to play in the Cedeno case – and in the widespread prejudice against the Irish that was endemic in this period. In the same week that the newspapers were reporting the Cambridge Terrace murder, the *Star* described a recent entertainment at the Colonists' Hall where 'Mr Bent's comical delineation of a Negro character kept the audience in a continual roar of laughter'.

Apart from two previous incidents of bad temper, Cedeno had shown no ill-will towards his fellow servants, and had been a quiet and apparently contented servant. Mrs Robinson had given him a good character. There was, said Joynt, something strange in this case, inexplicable from the evidence. There was no obvious motive for the murder. Though he made no plea of insanity, Joynt suggested that Cedeno had been seized by some unaccountable delusion, inducing uncontrollable rage, and that the jury should give him the benefit of the doubt and reduce the charge to manslaughter. In summing up, Joynt reminded the jury that Cedeno was 'of a race which was differently constituted as to passions to that of their own countrymen'. It was for the jury to decide whether it was murder or manslaughter.

Mr Justice Gresson then addressed the jury, commenting first on Joynt's remark that some people had blamed him for taking up Cedeno's defence. Gresson reminded the jury that it was the duty of every lawyer to give an accused person the best advice and assistance possible, since under English law the accused was presumed to be innocent until proven guilty. Gresson thought that Joynt had discharged his duty 'with temperateness, with candour, and ability'. He then warned the jury that they should not be influenced by anything they had heard outside the courtroom, or by any considerations of racial difference.

Gresson then explained the difference between murder and manslaughter, dwelling at length on the question of malice: 'Manslaughter is where the homicide is committed without any malice, where suddenly I snatch up some instrument at my hand under provocation and put the person who provoked me to death ... there must be some sufficient provocation, and there must not be time for the blood to cool.' He had expected Joynt to argue that Cedeno had suffered a sudden fit of madness or delusion, and that he was therefore not responsible for his actions. Where clear evidence of insanity was brought before the jury, a verdict of guilty by reason of temporary insanity was possible. But no such defence had been proposed, and Joynt had been right in not attempting a defence for which there were no grounds. Cedeno had shown no symptoms of insanity either before or after the murder. Gresson went on to elucidate the difference between general and particular malice, reminding the jury that the law presumes malice from the homicide itself. In his opinion, Cedeno had shown both general and particular malice towards the two servant girls, and there was no disputing the fact that he had attacked and killed Margaret Burke.

The jury retired for little more than 10 minutes and returned with a guilty verdict. Cedeno was asked through the interpreter if he had anything to say, but he replied that he did not. Gresson told him that he had sent Margaret Burke to meet her Maker without any warning or provocation, that he thought he had killed Catherine Glynn, and that he had threatened to kill his master. Cedeno had forfeited his life by the law of the land, and should use the short time left to him to make his peace with God. Gresson then donned the black cap and sentenced Cedeno to be hanged by the neck until he was dead.

Word soon spread from the courtroom to the crowd outside that Cedeno had been found guilty, as expected, and there were a few sporadic cheers, until the police warned those present that they might be charged with disorderly behaviour. They waited, however, to see Cedeno as he was removed from the courthouse. A cab was called, and as he was brought out the crowd hooted and groaned as it had on previous occasions. With some difficulty the cab moved off through a very hostile and threatening press of people, and turned the corner to cross the Victoria Bridge over the Avon River into the Market Place.

Then it stopped. Some part of the cab or its harness had broken, and the driver could not go on. The crowd, which had followed the cab from the courthouse, now surrounded it, with yet more hooting and shouting. The constable and detective with Cedeno in the cab now became fearful of what might happen next.

Fortunately, they were just outside the old police station and gaol in the Market Place. The gaoler, James Reston, with great presence of mind hustled Cedeno inside and, for his own safety, locked him in one of the former female cells. Constables guarded the door while a fresh cab was sought from the cabstand in front of the post office. As a *Press* reporter observed: 'Once [Cedeno was] inside, an immense crowd got around the place, and had it not been for the firmness and discretion evinced by Mr Reston, the gaoler, there is no doubt but that a very serious disturbance would have taken place.' The police waited until most of the crowd had drifted away, then put Cedeno in the second cab and set off for the railway station, to take him back to the Lyttelton Gaol. Christchurch had narrowly avoided an ugly incident that could have ended with a lynching.

Cedeno was executed at the Lyttelton Gaol at 8am on 5 April 1871. The date of his hanging had been kept secret, as with the execution of Swales, to thwart any morbidly curious onlookers. The sheriff and other officials went through to Lyttelton by a special train at 7.15 but did not walk up to the gaol until a few minutes before the time of execution. Cedeno was attended by two Catholic priests, Fathers Chervier and François Boibieux, and remained calm throughout. He died straight away, with no struggling.

Though Cedeno had made a sworn statement in January that Robinson had taunted him with such remarks as 'Black nigger, black heart', this statement was not given as evidence at the Supreme Court trial, and Joynt made no attempt to implicate Robinson in any provocation. Likewise, Joynt had not mentioned the story published in the newspapers, that the two Irish servants had been taunting Cedeno about his forthcoming marriage. This was only hearsay, and would not have been accepted as evidence, yet when placed alongside Robinson's alleged treatment of Cedeno this story at least raises the possibility of provocation. Cedeno had shown himself capable of brief bursts of anger, and his brooding resentment against his employer and his fellow servants seems to have erupted in a momentary paroxysm of violence, which he immediately regretted.

Such a case today would see the police making much more detailed enquiries about Cedeno's treatment by the Robinson family and his fellow servants, but it looks as if Robinson had made it clear that he did not want his family interrogated or involved in the case any more than was strictly necessary. The Supreme Court trial made no mention of the Robinson daughters as witnesses of the murder, much less call them to give evidence. Wealthy families in the nineteenth century often used their influence to keep their names out of the newspapers, but in this case it may have been the police not wanting to cause further distress to Mrs Robinson or her daughters. The key witness, Patrick Campbell, was in fact courting one of the daughters, and later married her.

The unfortunate Catherine Glynn was also later married, to a kindly cousin called George O'Malley, who did not mind her scarred face, but they had no children. It is said that she never got over the shock of Cedeno's attempt on her life.

The Robinson family paid for a tombstone to mark the grave of their former servant, Maggie Burke, but the sandstone developed a dark red stain that appeared to bleed after rain, and on the anniversary of her death. Some said it resembled a fist or closed hand. The stone with the bloodstained hand became one of Christchurch's legends, and people would visit the Barbadoes Street Cemetery simply to see this one grave. When the stone was vandalised in the 1960s and broken up, the source of the stain was found to be a patch of iron oxide or ironstone, which seeped reddish water when wet. The broken pieces disappeared when the cemetery was tidied up in the 1980s, and Maggie Burke's final resting place is no longer marked.

CHAPTER THIRTEEN

JANE MCLEOD: DEATH OF A ROWDY WOMAN

Half an hour before midnight on 14 January 1871 a labourer named John Coard, who lived in Tuam Street East, heard a woman scream outside his house. He opened the door and saw on his doorstep a neighbour, Jane McLeod, with her daughter, also called Jane. Mrs McLeod was moaning and appeared to be fainting so Coard helped her indoors. She then pulled her nightdress open and showed him two stab wounds on her breast. A man called John Hayes appeared in the doorway behind her, and Coard suggested he take her home while he sent for the police. They left immediately.

Constable Charles Rutledge was the first to respond, and went straight to Coard's house with the lad who had been sent to fetch the police. There he found Hugh McLeod, Jane's husband, sitting at a table, visibly upset and crying bitterly. When the constable asked him why he was weeping he said, 'They have done it for me now.' Coard told the constable that McLeod had stabbed his wife, so Rutledge took McLeod in charge 'on suspicion', and said he would have to come with him to see how she was. At McLeod's house, 100m away, they found Jane McLeod lying in bed in a room just off the kitchen. She had a large cut on her left breast, and there was blood on her nightdress and on the blankets. 'Policeman,' she said, 'send for a doctor,' so Rutledge sent for Dr Samuel Patrick. He then charged McLeod with stabbing his wife with intent to murder her, and gave him the usual caution.

Next on the scene was Inspector Peter Pender, who had known McLeod for some years. McLeod was sitting on a chair in the kitchen, with his head on the table. When Pender came in he got up and shook hands, and was going to say something when Pender advised him that it was best for him not to speak.

Dr Patrick arrived soon after Pender and found Jane McLeod in a state of partial collapse. Judging by the stains on the bed and on her nightdress she had lost a considerable amount of blood. He found two wounds on her chest, one between the fifth and sixth ribs beside the sternum, about 2½in (just over 6cm) in length, and the other, half that length, under her left breast. The wounds were connected: he could pass his finger from one to the other. Externally they seemed to have been incised by a sharp knife, but technically they were both puncture wounds.

Constable Rutledge was now able to run to the police depot and fetch the police wagon to take Jane McLeod to the hospital. He then took McLeod to the depot and searched him. McLeod was wearing a belt with a knife sheath but it was empty. The knife was later found on a footpath in Lichfield Street, about 40m from the McLeod house.

At the hospital Nurse Margaret Kindlysides, who was on duty when Mrs McLeod was admitted, noted that she was in 'a weak fainting state'. Dr Prins examined her and, like Dr Patrick, discovered that the two wounds were connected: 'Her hurried breathing and anxious countenance, the prostration that she was suffering, the character of the blood (it was frothy), and a careful cautious examination of the wound ... led me to believe that the wound had penetrated the cavity of the chest.' He considered all such wounds dangerous, however small, and he treated her accordingly, putting a lint dressing on it 'to keep the air out'. She was still 'perfectly conscious, rational, and sensible'. Over the next few days, however, her condition steadily worsened and she died five days later, on 19 February. Hugh McLeod, still in custody, was then charged with her murder.

His trial in the Supreme Court opened on 10 March 1871, before Mr Justice Gresson. McLeod, who pleaded not guilty, was defended by Thomas Joynt. Inspector Pender and Constable Rutledge gave their evidence, and agreed that McLeod did not appear to have been drinking. Pender had known him for some years and considered him 'a very respectable man ... a very quiet man'. He had been working 'up-country' at John Hall's Rakaia Station, and sent money back to his wife, who was caring for their four children. He knew that they did not live happily together, mainly on account of Jane McLeod's rowdy conduct: she had twice been imprisoned for vagrancy. (He did not mention that she had also been sent to prison for three months with hard labour in April 1870 for having committed a violent assault on her husband. When she was discharged on 11 July the *Police Gazette* described her as a 29-year-old prostitute with dark hair and blue eyes.)

About 18 months before, at the request of Magistrate Bowen and the Reverend Charles Fraser, Pender had visited the couple, and Hugh McLeod had asked his wife to go up-country with him, as 'he wanted to get her out of town'. She refused at first, then promised to go but failed to keep her word. Pender went to see her several times with McLeod to persuade her to go with him, but she would not leave. Some while after this she moved with her children to a house in Ferry Road, where Pender found Hugh McLeod one Sunday drinking with the other occupants: 'The inmates of the house were not of a good character. One of them was a reputed prostitute.' Pender told McLeod he would have nothing more to do with him, as he knew he should not be in such company.

From that time on, Pender said, McLeod had taken to drink, and he and his wife had 'got on very badly'. He would occasionally go away to get work and return for a short while, then go away again. She and the children lived in various brothels. They had not been long in the Tuam Street house, which McLeod had presumably rented to get his wife away from bad company.

McLeod's 10-year-old daughter, named after her mother, gave a lengthy description of what she could recall from the night of 14 February:

> My mother ... was very ill that day. She was in bed ... John Hayes was in our house that night. He was passing by and my father called him in. That was about eight o'clock. Hayes asked if he would have anything to drink, and my father said 'Yes, anything you like.' My mother said she did not want to bring any drink into the house. She said she didn't want Hayes in the house. She didn't say why ... my father asked me if I would go for some brandy, and I said I would not. Hayes gave him a £1 note and he went out and brought back a bottle of brandy and some change. My father asked my mother to take some. She refused, and he said if she didn't take it he would break the glass over her head. Then my father and Hayes went out for another bottle of brandy. Mrs McCormick came in. That bottle of brandy was drank [sic], too, by Mrs McCormick, Hayes and my father. My mother had some, but not much. They were drinking in the bedroom where my mother was lying. I was sitting on a small bedstead in the kitchen, opposite the bedroom door.

The girl thought the drinking session had lasted from 8.30 to 11.30, when Hugh McLeod came into the kitchen, removed his boots and vest, then took down a knife from a small shelf. As he walked into the bedroom holding it behind his back the child warned her mother. She replied that he wouldn't hurt her. But McLeod turned back to where young Jane was sitting, then went straight into the bedroom, still holding the knife behind him in his right hand.

> I saw him the whole time. He went up to the bed where my mother was and struck her in the left breast with the knife. I saw him strike her. My father then ran out through the kitchen into the street. I saw the knife in his hand when he was running out … Just as he was going out of the kitchen door he said, 'That will do you.' I am sure he said those words. He said them in a loud voice. My mother began to scream immediately on being struck. She kept up a continuous scream. I went out of the house, and saw my father standing at the corner of the gorse hedge. It was a moonlight night. The gorse fence was the corner of the East town belt [Fitzgerald Avenue].

When McLeod turned around Jane thought he was coming after her so she ran to John Coard's and woke him. 'When he got up and opened the door my mother was at the door. She had on a grey plaid dress and jacket. I didn't see my father after that until I saw Mr Coard take hold of him. Mr Coard told my father to come in and sit down. He went in. I went for Dr Prins. I didn't find him and went home. Mr Coard went for Dr Patrick.'

Having said that she would know the knife again, she identified it as the one she had seen her father sharpen on a large steel the night before. 'He cut his hand while sharpening it and my mother told him to put it away.' About an hour before this the couple had been quarrelling. When Jane McLeod asked her husband why he was sharpening the knife he said it was 'to cut the bands off wheat for a threshing machine he was working with'. About three months before, young Jane had heard Hugh McLeod threatening his wife. 'He said that he would either put a hand on her life or his own. He didn't say with what. That was all he said at the time.'

When cross-examined by Joynt, the girl said her father had been mostly at home for the last year or so, but he had been working up-country until the Saturday before the stabbing. He had been at home the whole of Sunday, Monday and Tuesday. She then insisted that her mother never drank by herself when her father was away, nor did she ever have men visiting her. She denied ever spending a week away from home: 'Nobody except me and the other three children lived with my mother while my father was up-country.'

Her father did not appear to be the worse for drink but he had been drinking plenty that evening. He and Hayes were just sitting talking about their work on some station where they had been: 'The conversation was actually going on in a perfectly friendly manner' until her father came out to get the knife. Mrs McCormick was leaving just as he did so. She had been there drinking the whole evening: 'Her little boy began to cry and wanted to go to bed, and she had to go.' In response to questioning by the judge, the girl said her parents had been on 'the most friendly terms' all through that Tuesday. She was sure there had been no quarrel between them. Indeed, her father's manner had been 'pleasant'. He was not excited or angry, and did not seem the worse for drinking so much brandy.

The next witness was John Hayes, who confirmed most of what young Jane McLeod had said, but disagreed with her point about the moonlight: 'There was no moon. It was not a dark night nor yet a bright one.' He also contradicted her statement that Mrs McLeod had not wanted to drink: she 'took her share of the brandy when it was brought without any hesitation'. One time she refused another drink and McLeod said he would break the glass over her head, but he had nothing in his hand. It looked to Hayes as if he said it in friendship, as a joke. She had made no reply. Hayes was certain there had been no quarrelling that night: in fact McLeod 'appeared to be quite jolly. He had been singing about a quarter of an hour before the blow was struck. There was no noise. Mrs McLeod was talking. We were all quiet.' John Coard confirmed that there was no moon that night, and said that McLeod had been very upset: '[H]e cried most bitterly when I took hold of him. He was behaving almost like a maniac; he was raving very much and making rambling statements.'

After further cross-examination of Dr Patrick, Joynt asked for an adjournment until the next day. The Crown prosecutor objected that this was simply in order to find another doctor to contradict Dr

Patrick's evidence, but Joynt insisted that he had no more witnesses to call other than those on his original list. He reminded the court that he had been at the bar since 10 that morning with no break for food or anything else. Mr Justice Gresson thought this a very reasonable request and adjourned the case until the following day.

Next morning Dr Prins gave evidence about his post-mortem examination of Jane McLeod's body. He had found the right side of the chest cavity filled with blood, and concluded that death had been caused by haemorrhage and exhaustion. With the exception of an enlarged liver and a flabby heart, the other organs appeared to be healthy. The knife wound had penetrated the right lung, which had been collapsed by the pressure of the blood collecting in the chest cavity. The wound in the lung had only 'a very slight appearance of inflammation'. He had expected the inflammation to be greater, 'from the fact of her being a dissolute, intemperate woman'. The enlargement of the liver had probably been caused by excessive drinking.

For the defence, Joynt then called a series of witnesses who painted a rather less charitable picture of the late Mrs McLeod than her daughter had given the court. John Buller, manager of the Rakaia Station, said he had known Hugh McLeod for about four years and had employed him for 18 months until the end of 1869. Soon after that he had had occasion to visit McLeod's address in Christchurch, near Papanui Road, where he found Jane McLeod at home and clearly drunk. There were two bottles and some glasses on the table and a strong smell of grog in the house. Another man was there, also drunk, sitting on a chair with his trousers unbuttoned.

As for McLeod himself, Buller said he had never met a more reliable and faithful worker, 'a quiet inoffensive man' who was 'kind and attentive to his wife – so much so as to attract my attention'. He had never seen McLeod the worse for drink, though he had many opportunities to get liquor if he wanted it.

William Holmes, fishmonger, told the court he had been a neighbour of Mrs McLeod for about two years:

I have seen her in bed with a man not her husband, repeatedly, and drinking going on, too, in the house. McLeod was working up country. On all those occasions Mrs McLeod partook of the drink. I saw her take it. I have seen the girl, Jane McLeod, present on these occasions. She often brought the drink, and sometimes Mrs McLeod went for it herself. I have seen the girl give her mother drink while she was in bed, and the man in bed with her ... At times there have been three or four women there, with men, chatting, drinking, and so on.

Holmes had often seen a man he knew named Gilmour at the McLeod house, the last time about a week before Mrs McLeod was wounded. 'I have seen him drinking and sitting in the house, but I never saw him in bed there. I have seen the girl Jane in the house frequently while Gilmour was there.' (The girl had denied knowing anyone of that name.) Whenever Hugh McLeod was away 'and money was sent down, Mrs McLeod was always drunk ... When she got money from him it was a common thing to see her drunk an hour afterwards.'

Under cross-examination, Holmes added that he had once seen a prostitute known as 'Sydney Liz' in the house, and at other times 'reputed prostitutes' named Clark and Dixon – probably Margaret Clarke and Theresa Dixon. McLeod had remarked to him that 'he had a good mind to turn Sydney Liz out' but she was one of his wife's favourite drinking companions.

Cab driver Thomas Crawford had no doubt that the house in Ferry Road where the McLeods had lived for a while was a brothel. He remembered driving Mrs McLeod and another man (not her husband) there from last year's Cattle Show on 9 November:

> They were both tipsy. They got out of the cab, and fell in the ditch. The neighbours came and lifted them up, and helped them towards the house. I have been in the house frequently. Men would come asking for it, and I would drive them [there]. Sometimes the men whom I took there sent me for drink, and sometimes the little girl Jane McLeod would go. I am sure the girl was present when the drink was being consumed.

Another cabman, James Hunter, told a very similar story. He had driven men to the house and had seen as many as five men there, drinking with Mrs McLeod, often with the little girl present.

The Reverend Charles Fraser, a Presbyterian minister, told the court he had known the McLeod family for about 12 years. He recalled obtaining charitable aid for them about three or four years before, when there was sickness in the family: 'McLeod was a very quiet, honest, and worthy man.' About two years before he had come to Fraser 'in great distress of mind on account of his wife's conduct'. Fraser had gone to their house and spoken to them both. McLeod wanted to get her employment at the same station where he was working, to get her away from her associates. When they moved to Ferry Road, McLeod had told Fraser that it was 'with the view of getting her as far as possible from town', but the minister was sure that Hugh McLeod did not know the place was a brothel. He had warned McLeod once or twice to be very careful about drink, and to think of his family's welfare. Mrs McLeod had never had anything to say to the minister.

The last two witnesses for the defence were Dr Courtney Nedwill and Dr John Frankish, who had been asked to examine the deceased, to prove the correctness or otherwise of the prosecution's medical evidence. Nedwill was surprised to find almost no inflammation around the wound on the lung. Given Mrs McLeod's drinking habits, and the four days that had elapsed since the stabbing, he would have expected much more inflammation by the time she died. He surmised that the haemorrhage had come from the intercostal arteries cut by the knife, and that the accumulation of blood in the chest cavity had collapsed the lung. This need not have been fatal, as he had known patients to live for years in such a state, but the absence of inflammation around the wound on the lung 'would be contrary to all my experience and reading'. He then suggested that the cut on the lung could have been caused by a slip of the knife during the post-mortem.

Dr Frankish agreed with Nedwill's analysis: 'A wound like this would be sure to inflame acutely from the action of the air communicated through the wall of the chest, because the air would set up decomposition.' Under further questioning by the judge, Frankish said that such a wound might accelerate death, but not necessarily cause it. The death of Mrs McLeod could have been caused by a blood clot on the brain, quite unrelated to the stabbing.

In his final address to the jury, Joynt reviewed the evidence in detail, 'not forgetting a single point that could be urged upon the attention of the jury in favour of the accused'. In conclusion he asked the jury to return a verdict, not of manslaughter, but of guilty or not guilty. Mr Justice Gresson agreed, and directed the jury that as there was no evidence of provocation they must return a verdict of guilty or not guilty on the charge of wilful murder. For a guilty verdict they had to be satisfied beyond any reasonable doubt that it was the hand of the accused that inflicted the wound, and that the injury had accelerated the death of his wife.

The jury retired for three-quarters of an hour, then returned with a verdict of guilty but with a strong recommendation for mercy. When Gresson asked, 'On what grounds?' the foreman replied, 'On account of the previous good character he has received, and the provocation that he has received from his wife.' The judge made a note of this. The registrar then asked McLeod his age: the answer was 34. (On 11 March the *Press* had described him as 'an elderly man [who] seemed impressed with the awful nature of his position'.) The registrar recited the usual formula – that McLeod had pleaded not guilty and put himself upon the verdict of a jury, and that jury had found him guilty. When asked if he had anything to say, McLeod said in a low voice that he did not.

Gresson reminded the prisoner that he had taken the life of a fellow creature and sent his wife to meet her Maker without a moment's notice, 'and with all her sins unrepented for'. He had not the least doubt that McLeod bitterly repented of what he had done, and even now suffered deeply for it. However, having been found guilty, his life was now forfeit and the judge had no power to remit that sentence of the law. The jury had recommended mercy, and Gresson said he would have 'great pleasure' in forwarding that recommendation to the government, but there was no guarantee that it would succeed. In the meantime McLeod should make his peace with God.

The judge donned the black cap and sentenced McLeod to death by hanging. The newspaper reporters noted that 'His Honour was visibly affected while passing sentence'. McLeod had throughout the trial 'appeared to feel his position most acutely', and his 'quiet subdued demeanour' in the dock had presented a marked contrast to that of the previous accused murderer, Simon Cedeno.

Within a few days a petition was being circulated in Christchurch, prepared by Thomas Joynt and signed by Dean Jacobs, the Reverend Charles Fraser and several other worthy citizens. Addressed to His Excellency Sir George Bowen, KCMG, Governor of New Zealand, it stated that Hugh McLeod, now lying in Lyttelton Gaol for the murder of his wife, had for many years maintained 'an excellent character as an industrious, quiet, inoffensive man'. The petitioners claimed that he had been 'led into habits of intemperance for the last eighteen months through the bad conduct of his wife and the temptations of her paramours and other evil associates', that he had committed the crime under circumstances of great provocation, and that the jury had made a strong recommendation to mercy.

This petition was successful, and Hugh McLeod was released from prison later in 1871. Since there is no record of his death in New Zealand, it seems likely that he took his children to Australia to make a fresh start there.

This trial sparked a spectacular stoush among the medical fraternity of Christchurch. Dr Prins was outraged that his competence had been questioned by two younger doctors, and refused to allow Nedwill or Frankish anywhere near the hospital. The provincial government instead appointed Dr Powell and Mr Parkerson as the hospital's visiting surgeons. When asked whether the hospital's surgical staff needed to be increased, Dr Prins had said he saw no necessity as he could perform all the department's work himself. The quarrel became public in October 1871 with the publication of correspondence between Drs Nedwill and Frankish and the provincial government, in which they called for a public inquiry into Mrs McLeod's post-mortem. They alleged negligence by Dr Prins for not having examined all of the vital organs. Nedwill failed to get his inquiry, but Prins was later persuaded to relent and allow the younger doctors to rejoin the hospital staff.

The McLeod case was not forgotten, however, and may help to explain the continued bickering and conflict at the hospital throughout the 1870s and 1880s. Given the state of medical knowledge at the time, before Pasteur's work with bacteria was widely known or accepted, it never occurred to any of the doctors that Dr Patrick and Dr Prins had probably worsened the haemorrhage and introduced infection by inserting their non-sterile fingers into Jane McLeod's wound.

CHAPTER FOURTEEN

ASSORTED ASSAULTS AND BIGAMIES

DOMESTIC BLISS.
SCENE – THE KITCHEN
COOK – 'Who was that at the door, Mary?'
MARY – 'Oh! Such a nice gentleman with moustachers. He's a'writin a letter in the drawing room. He says he's an old schoolfeller of master just come from Ingia.'
SCENE – THE HALL
The nice-spoken gentleman is seen departing with what greatcoats and other trifles he may have laid his hands upon.

John Leech, *Four Hundred Humorous Illustrations*, 2nd edn, 1862

T he cabmen and bus drivers of 1870s Christchurch were regarded with deep suspicion by most respectable citizens, and with good reason. Although there were some perfectly honest and law-abiding cabbies, collectively they were notorious for their bad language, hard drinking, furious driving and readiness to use their fists in an argument. They also knew where all of the brothels were, and, as we have seen, could sometimes be found drinking with prostitutes and their customers. Cabmen always risked having their licence from the city council cancelled if they got into trouble with the police, but the demand for transport was such that they were nearly always back on the streets within a few months or a year. Many of the assault cases coming before the Magistrate's Court involved cabmen or drivers.

The career of Archibald Hammil neatly demonstrates why cabmen enjoyed such a poor reputation. He owned an omnibus and normally plied the route between Springfield and Waltham roads. In December 1871 he appeared before Magistrate Bowen with a known prostitute, Margaret Guerin, on a charge of having indecently exposed themselves on St Albans Road. Witnesses left the court in no doubt that the two of them had been 'misbehaving' in full view of anyone passing by. Margaret Guerin said she knew nothing whatever of the matter, having been picked up by Hammil when she was 'in a state of insensibility from drunkenness'. She was dismissed with a stern caution but Hammil was fined £5.

Less than two months later Hammil was back in court facing a much more serious charge. There had been a collision between two omnibuses in High Street near Cathedral Square, as a result of a race between Falloon's bus, which normally ran between the post office and the railway station, and the one owned by Hammil, which was being driven by a man called Harris. They had been racing, and in the collision Harris's passenger, one Mr Miller, had been thrown onto the road and 'rendered insensible'. Constable Philip Thoreau had taken him to be treated by Dr Patrick in Cashel Street, and while they were there someone dashed in to say that Hammil was driving his omnibus at speed around the High Street Triangle.

Constable Thoreau ran to the Triangle, where he seized the horses' reins, but Hammil, who was 'mad drunk', struck him several times with his whip and the constable was forced to let go. He pursued Hammil but was unable to catch him; he was not arrested until that evening. Charles Griffin testified that Hammil had driven three times around the Triangle 'at a furious pace'. He also corroborated the constable's account of the episode. Magistrate Bowen asked if Hammil still held a licence for his omnibus, and when Sergeant Horneman said no, Bowen replied that he was very glad to hear it. He had already advised the city council that Hammil was unfit to have a licence, as he had four convictions – for drunkenness, disorderly behaviour, indecent conduct and assault on his wife, for which he had been bound over for six months to keep the peace. His driving 'was fraught with great danger to the public safety'. Hammil's only excuse was that he was very drunk at the time and did not know what he was doing. Bowen took a dim view of his assault on the constable, who was only doing his duty and trying to protect the public from harm, and sentenced Hammil to two months in prison with hard labour.

Archibald Hammil appears to have kept out of trouble for the next few years but he was back in court in December 1875 for having violently assaulted his wife, Sarah, yet again. He was bound over to keep the peace for six months. Sureties of £50 from himself and £25 from another were demanded, with the alternative of 14 days in prison. A month later, however, he was charged with deserting his wife and leaving her without sufficient means of support. It appeared that Sarah had come home the previous Saturday night and found the door locked. Hammil refused to let her in. She returned on the Sunday, and again he barred the door. He relented only after she had gone to the police and laid a complaint against him. Sarah claimed she had been driven to drink by his cruel treatment. The magistrate said he would dismiss the case, as she was living at home once more. Hammil then piped up to say that he would like to have a separation from his wife. Sarah said she was agreeable to that, so long as he made suitable provision for her. The magistrate advised them to see a solicitor and get a deed of separation drawn up.

Christopher Bowen was always willing to give criminals a second chance if they promised to reform. In January 1872 Alexander Walker appeared before him on a charge of violently assaulting his wife. The evidence showed that a serious attack had taken place, but she blamed it entirely on his recently contracted drinking habit. They had been married for 12 or 13 years, and he never annoyed her except when he had had too much to drink. Walker assured the magistrate that he regretted his lapse, and promised to take the pledge. Bowen dismissed the case, urging them both to 'let by-gones be by-gones', but warning Walker that if he appeared again on such a charge he would be dealt with severely.

A much more serious case of assault was heard in the Supreme Court before Mr Justice Gresson in January 1874. Newlyweds Charles and Amy Mears lived in a house on Lincoln Road, and had a small shop some 100m away. He also earned extra money by helping to milk the cows for a nearby milkman, Henry Manaton. On Christmas Eve 1873, a Wednesday, Charles came home about 4 o'clock and was met at the door by his wife, who had a cloth wrapped around her head. She said, 'That man has been here again.' She took him through to the bedroom and showed her husband 'marks of blood on various articles'. Her face and neck were badly bruised and swollen. The intruder had threatened her with a knife and tried to rape her, but she had resisted. He had seized her by the throat and squeezed her so hard that she began to bleed from her mouth and nostrils 'and thought she was going to die'.

Her assailant was identified as Antonio Jansen, alias Theodore Beauman, who had recently come to Canterbury as a crew member on the immigrant ship *Columbus*. He was recognised on Lincoln Road close to the time of the assault by a former *Columbus* passenger, Mary Jane Lawren. Several other witnesses identified him at the scene, including labourer John Cassin, who was working on Mill Road and living nearby in a tent with a fellow workmate named Williams. Jansen had come to their tent on the Monday looking for work, and had returned on the Tuesday, when they took him in. He stayed that night in the tent but went away on the Wednesday morning, saying he had to meet a Mr Hall about a job.

Henry Manaton sometimes helped his father, John, who had a blacksmith's forge close to the Mears' shop. He recalled that Jansen had come into the forge that Wednesday and said he was waiting for a Mr Hall there. He sat down and they talked. He pointed to the Mears' house and asked, 'Who lives there?' Manaton had replied, 'Mrs Mears.' Jansen then asked, 'Is she married?' Manaton said, 'Yes, about three months ago.' Jansen then said, 'She's got a sister who wears spectacles and comes up and down the road.' Manaton agreed. Jansen's next words were: 'I'll be off over and wait till I see him.' Manaton did not know who he meant, but watched as Jansen walked across the road to the Mears' house. He did not see him again until he was taken away in the police van the same evening.

Amy Mears told the court that Jansen had come to the house on the Monday asking for her husband, but when she said he was milking, Jansen had gone away. When she mentioned this to her husband he was puzzled, as he had never met or spoken to anyone of that name. Jansen had returned on the Wednesday afternoon, entering through the back door. When she asked what he was doing there he said her husband had told him to wait in the house until he returned. She did not believe this and felt afraid, whereupon he seized her and pushed her into the bedroom, where the assault took place.

Much of the evidence concerned the white shirt Jansen had been wearing when he left Manaton, which he was not wearing when he returned to Cassin's tent about 5pm. When Inspector Pender came to question him that evening he was wearing it concealed underneath a Crimean shirt. (Such garments, popular with working men and with miners, were made of grey wool and had a neckband rather than a collar.) The white shirt had bloodstains on it, and this was the crucial evidence that linked Jansen to the crime.

Dr Julius Haast, director of the newly founded Canterbury Museum, was the interpreter at the Supreme Court trial of Antonio Jansen, at which 'evidence was given which showed that an assault of the most savage and brutal nature had been committed'. The jury, without retiring, returned a verdict of guilty. Gresson told Jansen that he had been convicted of 'a very gross outrage upon a respectable female', and regretted that the law did not allow him to pass a much heavier sentence. He gave Jansen two years with hard labour in the Lyttelton Gaol, where we shall meet him again later in this chapter.

Cases of bigamy were not as common as might be expected in colonial times, when so many men were moving about in search of work or working away from home on the goldfields or on road or railway construction. Nor were they always as straightforward as they appeared at first sight. Some of the bigamy cases of the 1870s suggest that there were faults on both sides of these unhappy marital disputes. They also reveal how quickly and carelessly some people got married. Our first example involves one of the witnesses, and indeed a key participant, from the Cedeno murder case of 1870.

John Price, as we have seen, was employed as a groom at the Cambridge Terrace house rented by the wealthy runholder William 'Ready Money' Robinson, and had helped to restrain Cedeno after he had stabbed Maggie Burke. In October 1873 Price was in the Christchurch Supreme Court, where he had given evidence only three years earlier, to face a charge of bigamy, or, to be precise, a breach of the 1854 Marriage Act. He pleaded not guilty and was defended by William Travers, one of New Zealand's rising barristers of the late nineteenth century. (He was a co-founder of the New Zealand Institute and the Wellington Botanic Gardens. Presumably Robinson was paying his fee.)

The Crown prosecutor first submitted copies of the *New Zealand Gazette* to establish the appointment of Burrell Parkerson as the registrar of births, deaths and marriages for the Christchurch district, and Travers at once objected, saying that such an appointment was under the hand of the governor. Thomas amended his submission to avoid any further argument. He then submitted the marriage certificate of John Birch (also known as John Price) to Elizabeth Stone at Nelson in 1855. Travers again objected, saying that this was a copy in the form of the 1858 Marriage Act Amendment, and not the original 1854 legislation. Gresson overruled this objection, and allowed the certificate to be put in as evidence.

Mary Gough told the court she had been a domestic servant at Robinson's house, where she got to know Price, and left in order to get married. She went to live with her mother in Lyttelton until the wedding, which was arranged for 25 July 1873, six weeks later. On that day, when they went to give notice to the registry office in Christchurch, Price was asked if he had been married before and he said no. He said he was a horse-breaker, 36 years of age, who had lived in Christchurch for 15 years. The wedding was to take place at 'the Roman Catholic Church', most likely the wooden predecessor to the Cathedral of the Blessed Sacrament. Price signed the declaration, and the registrar gave them each a copy of the certificate for marriage.

But the wedding never went ahead. The engagement ended when Mary Gough heard that Price already had a wife. She claimed he had never told her he had been married before.

Evidence was then heard from Samuel Stone, formerly a Nelson farmer, whose daughter Elizabeth had married Price in 1855. Stone said that his real name was Birch. They had lived together as man and wife for a year or so, and a child was born, but Price then left her and went to work on Robinson's Cheviot Hills Station. Stone and his daughter had come down to Canterbury and lived at Woodend, but after five or six years she had moved to Blenheim. Stone had stayed at Woodend for the past decade, and occasionally saw Price, who had several times asked how his daughter was. So he knew where she was, and what she was doing, as well as her father did: 'I believe he saw her at my place. I heard he did. I never wished him to see her. I would rather have kept him away from her.' He recalled that Price had once given him a watch to give to his daughter.

The defence case was that no second marriage had taken place, and therefore there had been no breach of the Marriage Act. Price and his first wife had been separated for more than a decade, and all contact had ceased more than seven years before. The Crown had failed to produce any evidence to show that the prisoner had known his wife was still alive.

Mr Justice Gresson suddenly declared that there was sufficient evidence to go before the jury, who retired briefly and returned with a verdict of not guilty. Gresson then discharged Price with this parting warning: 'Although you have got off, I would advise you not to attempt such a thing again.'

In April 1874 one Moses Hymus appeared in the Christchurch Supreme Court charged with having married one Mary Elizabeth Dady on 12 December 1873, while his previous wife, Elizabeth Gortage, was still alive. Detective Sergeant Feast told the court that when he went to arrest him, Hymus had said that Mary Dady knew he was a married man, that he behaved well towards her and did not let her want for anything. Questioned by Thomas Joynt for the defence, Feast said that on the way to the police depot Hymus had remarked that his former wife was living with another man, so he did not see why he should not take another wife. Feast added that Elizabeth Gortage was living with a man named Parker, with whom she had had a child. He recalled that, two or three years ago, she had sued Hymus for maintenance in the Magistrate's Court, and he had promised to provide a home for her if she came back to him. She had refused, however, saying she would never live with him, and the case was dismissed. Hymus had a fruit shop in Christchurch but was up-country harvesting when Feast found him. The detective sergeant thought him a sober, industrious man but 'a little weak-minded'.

Elizabeth Gortage then gave evidence that her daughter, Elizabeth Maria, was married to Hymus at the Wesleyan Chapel in Durham Street on 26 December 1870, by the Reverend William Kirk. The couple had lived together for only a week before Hymus went up-country to look for work:

For three months after that we never knew where he was. He came to my house when he returned. He lived at my house with my daughter. He lived with her for two months. He went away for six months. We did not know where he was ... He promised to write but he never did. They never lived happily together. The day after the marriage, he wanted her to take the name of Townley, and she refused. He asked her to go up the country with him, but she refused, because he ill-used her so. He struck her in my house. On two occasions, my daughter prosecuted him for maintenance ... He had a former wife before he married my daughter. We heard it for a fact ... I only state this from hearsay.

Mary Elizabeth Dady was then called upon to give evidence, and told the court that she was married to Moses Hymus on 12 December 1873 by the Reverend Macfarlane at Park Road, Addington. She had lived with him as his wife for three weeks. He had told her he had been married before, but was divorced. However, people had met her in the street and told her he was not divorced, and that his first wife was still alive, so she was living in sin. She then left him and went into service at the Oxford Hotel in the Market Place.

In response to questions from defence counsel Thomas Joynt she added that she had come to Canterbury as a single woman on the government immigration scheme and had no relatives in New Zealand. She was 20 but had said that she was 21, as Hymus had told her she could not get married otherwise. He claimed he had left his first wife because she used to drink, and that he had gone through the courts to get a divorce as he found her intolerable to live with.

Henry Mainyard had come out in the same ship as Mary Dady and had been a witness at their marriage in December 1873. After that they lived in High Street as man and wife. Mary had known Hymus for only a fortnight before the wedding. Hymus had told Mainyard he had a legal separation from his first wife and could get the papers any day by applying to the court.

Joynt's defence was very simple. The second marriage was null and void because they were married without obtaining the registrar's certificate, and the Reverend Macfarlane was not registered as an officiating minister under the Marriages Act Amendment of 1858. The certificate he had issued had not been signed by him, the couple or the witnesses. It had not been produced by the Crown prosecutor, Thomas Duncan, but by Mary Dady herself.

Gresson said that, however unwilling he felt, in view of the clear moral guilt of the prisoner, he must allow the point raised by the defence. When Duncan admitted that Mr Macfarlane's name did not appear in the *Gazette*'s list of officiating ministers, Gresson drily observed, 'That, I presume, is the reason you did not produce it.' He then directed the jury to return a verdict of not guilty, which they did.

It is very rare to find first-hand testimony of everyday life in the Lyttelton Gaol, or the treatment of prisoners by their warders, but an inquest in July 1874 opens for us a door that was normally kept shut and guarded. The deceased was an old soldier, John Bickell, who, it was alleged, had died after being assaulted by warder John Neill. Dr William Donald, the Lyttelton coroner and resident magistrate, conducted the post-mortem examination, with assistance from Drs Rouse and Macdonald. On one leg they found the scar of a very old bayonet wound, and a similar scar from an old injury on the other leg. The lungs were healthy, the right one showing signs of a longstanding pleurisy with adhesions between lung and ribs. The heart was very fatty but the liver was large and healthy, as were the intestines. However, the spleen was 'enormously large', very soft and broken in texture, and the portion of the stomach lying close by the spleen was 'of a dark chocolaty colour'. Dr Donald concluded that the death had been from natural causes, namely a diseased spleen and a weak heart.

The first of the witnesses was a fellow prisoner, Walter Johnston, who said he had seen Neill go into the passage leading to the solitary confinement cell and heard him unlock it. He heard Bickell call out, 'Oh, let me alone.' Then there was what sounded like a kick – 'it sounded dull, as if on a body' – and a groan from Bickell. When Johnston mentioned this to other prisoners they seemed quite unconcerned: 'Oh, that's nothing.' One man said he had seen the warders drag Bickell out by his feet and bump his head on the stone steps leading into the yard. Another young man said he had seen Neill kick Bickell. On hearing that Bickell had been taken to the infirmary, Johnston had reported what he had heard to James Reston, the head gaoler. He was apprehensive about doing so, since he was serving a long sentence for larceny and knew that 'if prisoners report they have to put up with the consequences'.

Alfred Jones remembered 15 June, as Neill had told him to take Bickell's breakfast to him in the infirmary. That was after roll-call at 8am. Bickell was still in bed, and, according to Jones, Neill told him to get up. Bickell said he could not, whereupon the warder 'ran and made a kick at him, and struck him on the right side, he then pulled the blankets off him and pulled the bed from under him', leaving Bickell on the damp floor, which had just been washed: 'He left him quite naked without even a shirt on.'

Bickell, who had been sick for some days, had moaned that Neill would be the death of him, and that he was too ill to get up. Jones said he had never before seen Bickell refuse to obey an order from a warder. Jones had to depart to join his work gang, and Bickell was left lying on the floor. Like Johnston, Jones had not reported the incident because he was serving a long sentence and feared retribution from the warders.

Richard Wood, in prison for robbery, told the inquest that he had been in a cell with Bickell on 2 June when warders Neill and McDade told Bickell to take his bed out into the passage. Bickell, who was shirtless, had only a blanket around his shoulders. McDade pulled the blanket off and struck him, while Neill kicked him. Bickell shouted 'Murder!' and begged them not to kill him. Wood shouted out that it was a shame for them to kick Bickell: 'I am quite sure both warders kicked him.' Again, he did not report the matter as he was due to go for trial.

Antonio Jansen, the immigrant convicted of assault and attempted rape, had also spent some time in the infirmary in June, and one morning saw Neill go into the ward where Bickell was sleeping. A short time later he heard Bickell shout 'Oh!' very loudly, as if in pain. Neill left, and a little while later Bickell came out with blood on his arm: 'The man was ill at the time. He told me his inside was gone.'

Charles Thompson, a convicted forger, had the job of sweeping out the cells. Two days before Bickell was removed to the infirmary he heard Neill tell Bickell to get up and wash himself. Bickell said he was dying and wanted to see the doctor. 'Immediately after this, I heard a blow. I cannot say whether it was from the hand or foot; it sounded like a slap.' (Here Thompson struck his hands sharply together.) Bickell then started to groan 'in a frightful manner'. Neill came out and shut the door:

> A short time before that, I cannot tell the date, as we never see a newspaper, but it was about a fortnight, I was called in to sweep out the solitary cells. I went into Bickell's cell. He had no shirt on. He held up his left arm, and pointing with his right to his heart said to Warder Neill, 'That is where you struck me'. Bickell said he would tell the doctor. He also murmured he was dying. Warder Neill said ... he would have none of his old soldier's tricks there. I swept the cell and came out.

Thompson had never seen Bickell 'use any violence' towards the warders, despite their cruelty. He also mentioned that Bickell had lately been 'very dirty in his habits' and he did not 'consider him in his right mind'. Thompson had something else to say. About five weeks before, when he had been in Bickell's cell, Neill had told Bickell to take out his slop-bucket and look smart about it. Bickell was slow and Neill had pushed him into the passage, making him spill the contents. Thompson was sent to get a mop and bucket of water and Neill told Bickell to clean up the mess but he refused, saying, 'You can do what you like with me, I do not care.' According to Thompson, Neill then pushed Bickell over the steps 'in a most brutal manner' and shoved him twice across the yard. Bickell took all of this meekly.

Several other prisoners had similar stories, one stating that he had seen Neill strike Bickell several times with his bunch of keys. Another said he had often had conversations with Bickell and had concluded that he was mentally unsound, as he used to cry out at night and tear up his clothes. (This may explain why he was often without a shirt.) The other warders treated him kindly but Neill had no patience with him.

Neill was then asked to explain himself. He maintained that Bickell was a very difficult and refractory prisoner, dirty in his habits. It was often necessary to wash out his cell in the mornings and change his bedding. He would refuse to get up, and that was when Neill would pull the bed out from under him: 'The bed, blankets and floor would sometimes be in a frightful beastly state.' He would be taken out into the yard for exercise while his cell was cleaned. He often refused to clean it himself. Neill claimed never to have hit Bickell 'with my keys, foot, or fist'. In response to a question he said he had no specific orders about what to do when a prisoner refused to get out of bed.

Dr Donald told the inquest that although Bickell had been in apparently good health when he came to the gaol, he was always complaining that he was dying. After 20 minutes' deliberation the inquest jury returned a verdict of death by natural causes, but added the rider that warder Neill had used 'undue severity', and that Bickell was of 'unsound mind'.

That last statement naturally raises the question of what Bickell was doing in the Lyttelton Gaol in 1874 if he was suffering from mental illness. In the early days of the settlement Canterbury's mentally ill had been housed in the Lyttelton Gaol, in the same dormitories as hardened criminals. Under Edward Seager's enlightened leadership some attempt had been made to segregate the two, but since the opening of the Sunnyside Asylum in 1863 anyone certified by two doctors as being of unsound mind had been sent there rather than to Lyttelton. Bickell may have been one of those unfortunate borderline cases who had deteriorated while in custody, and was merely thought of as a troublesome malingerer, rather than mentally ill.

The construction of a new prison at Addington, and its enlargement by Benjamin Mountfort in 1870 according to the best principles of Victorian prison design, at last removed the female prisoners from Lyttelton and temporarily eased the chronic overcrowding at the old gaol.

A few months before he left the Lyttelton Gaol to become the first keeper at Sunnyside, Seager had written a long letter to the *Lyttelton Times*, which was published on 11 April 1863. Much of what he wrote was still relevant a decade later. He was scathing about the overcrowding and poor layout of the gaol, which made it impossible to keep prisoners of different classes of offences segregated. The prison had been added to over the years in a haphazard manner, as more accommodation was needed, and its form had become 'nearly useless'. Noting that the arrangements in a prison 'should tend to the reformation of the criminal', Seager added that the selection of warders was of great importance:

> A warder having such close intercourse with the prisoners has necessarily a great influence for good or evil over them. In order that he should have the former, he should be a keen, discerning man, possessed of courage, tact, industry and good temper, and one who has a moderate education, and, above all, a long experience in police or gaol duties.

Seager laid particular stress on this last qualification, which allowed the warder to detect 'those thousand and one devices by which every old hand is prepared to evade work, and annoy those in authority over him'. He then went on to describe some of the tricks practised by old offenders, many of them designed to get on the sick list, such as 'eating soap and licking the whitewash from the walls, to give the appearance of a bilious attack, swallowing tobacco juice, which brings on temporary palpitation of the heart, and pricking the gums to counterfeit spitting of blood. I have even known a prisoner to swallow pounded glass to bring on symptoms of a serious nature.' Female prisoners commonly became particularly unruly on the days when warders were wearing dress uniform, 'with express intention of damaging them'. These, Seager concluded, were

> the most common and best known of their plans for annoying the officials. I refrain from mentioning others, as I am by no means desirous of instructing future rogues through the medium of your columns. It is therefore obvious that if a man is not by experience acquainted with all these dodges he is not fit for the part of a warder.

Warder Neill's reference to 'old soldier's tricks' suggests that he believed Bickell was feigning illness in order to get breakfast in bed in the infirmary, but the testimony of the other prisoners tends to indicate that Bickell was not only unwell but also unhinged and incontinent. His behaviour sounds more like that of some of the inmates at Sunnyside. Neill's brutal treatment of this sick man may have been exceptional, if other prisoners said that most of the warders treated Bickell with kindness. When set alongside Seager's requirements for the ideal prison warder, Neill plainly lacked discernment, tact and good temper. One wonders how many other prison warders of the 1870s were like him.

CHAPTER FIFTEEN

DEATHS OF CHILDREN, 1875

REWARD OF MERIT.
Ragged Urchin – 'Please, give dad a short pipe.'
Barman – 'Can't do it. Don't know him.'
Ragged Urchin – 'Why, he gets drunk here every Saturday night.'
Barman – 'Oh! Does he, my little dear? Then 'ere's a nice long 'un, with
a bit of wax at the end.'

John Leech, *Four Hundred Humorous Illustrations*, 2nd edn, 1862

Late in the afternoon of Saturday 9 January 1875 John Bailey, a lad who lived in St Davids Street, Lyttelton, was driving some cows in from a paddock above the town. While pursuing a cow that had strayed from the herd, he noticed a white handkerchief hanging on the gorse hedge of the Reverend Frederick Pember's orchard on

Ripon Street, near the cemetery. He told his friends Alfred Simmonds and Thomas Rouse that he had also seen what looked like a drunken man lying under the gorse. Rouse ran off to fetch his elder brother Richard, while Bailey and Simmonds, after they had retrieved the wandering cow, went back for a closer look. Through a gap in the hedge they could see the body of a girl. Richard Rouse then came up with another lad named Knowles. When he saw blood on the girl's face he told his brother to go and fetch the police at once. The boys waited beside the hedge until Constable James Wallace arrived. As he later informed the inquest,

> On looking through the hedge, I saw the body of the deceased lying under the gorse fence, with the face covered in blood. On getting through the fence, I saw a large cut-wound commencing and running round from the left ear and round the throat. I put my hand upon her stomach, which was uncovered, and found that she was dead; the body was quite cold. The clothes were turned up to the middle of the body. The position she was lying in was on her back, her legs were apart, lying straight down. Her arms lay by her side; her right cheek was lying on the ground. I found a pair of drawers under her right thigh; there were blood marks upon them; the buttons which fastened them was pulled off and hanging by a thread ... I also found a man's pocket-handkerchief under her right shoulder; this had blood on it, as if made by wiping a knife on it. Her hat was lying about four feet off from where her head was. Two school picnic tickets were lying near her right hand.

The victim was soon identified as Isabella Thompson, who was due to celebrate her twelfth birthday in two weeks' time.

Bad news spreads quickly in a small community, and this was shocking news. Isabella was the daughter of a well-known shipwright, John Blair Thompson. He told the police he had last seen his daughter shortly before 5pm that day, in Dampiers Bay, on her way to the Colonists' Hall to buy tickets for her parents to attend the school picnic. He described her as healthy and strong, laughing as she danced down the hill. 'I next saw her at the police station, dead.'

As people recalled what they had seen that afternoon, they came to the Lyttelton police station to offer their assistance. Annie Rouse came that evening to tell Sergeant-Major O'Grady that she had seen a strange man come out of Ripon Street and into Oxford Street between 5.30 and 6pm. She had a good view from the bow window of her father's house on that corner. She wondered what he was doing there, and took note of his clothing. He went down Oxford Street and hurried towards the railway station. Mrs Susannah Toomey had also seen him, coming out of the parsonage grounds into Ripon Street. She noted that he steadied himself on the post and rail fence before staggering down Oxford Street to the railway station.

The body of Isabella Thompson had been brought down to the police station about 6.30pm. Sergeant-Major O'Grady took the body to the morgue, noticing that the dead girl's clothes had a large amount of dry gorse stuck to them.

More information came to the police next day, a Sunday. John Hall and Robert Russell, carpenters working on a government contract, had been on the 6pm train that left Lyttelton the night before. A man had got into their carriage and said, 'The Government men ought to go out in the horse box and leave room for the public.' Russell had replied by asking why the man did not wash his hands before he spoke to them: they had blood on them, especially the left one. Russell knew the man as John Mercer, a seaman. Mercer replied that he had been killing a sheep. Hall also noticed fresh blood on his nose and on his right cheek below the eye. Both Hall and Russell made sworn statements to the Lyttelton police.

John Skeet, a seaman living in Oxford Street, told the police he had been leaning on the railings of Baker's stables about 5.40 on the Saturday afternoon. The train had come in and the crossing gates had been opened and closed. Looking up towards the parsonage he saw a man shaking his coat. He appeared to be tipsy, so Skeet kept watching as he came down the hill. He seemed to be in a hurry. Skeet thought he saw blood on his cheek.

The most damning information came from another seaman,

Nathan Percy, who had just been discharged from the schooner *Canterbury* after a voyage from Westport to Lyttelton. Mercer had been a member of the crew but had transferred to the *Cleopatra*. Percy said he had met Mercer in Oxford Street about 3pm on the Saturday:

> I went up to him and asked him if he was going to Christchurch. He said, 'I want nothing to do with you'. He had previously spoken about going to Christchurch with me. He then said, 'I want to go with someone else; I want to get a girl, and if I can't get one here, I can get one in Christchurch. And if I don't get what I want I will cut her weasand [gullet] or her throat.'

All this was more than enough for the police to act on. First thing on the morning of 11 January, Detective Harry Feast and Sergeant-Major O'Grady went out to the schooner *Cleopatra*, anchored in the harbour, and went aboard. Mercer came forward to the ladder, and O'Grady noticed that when he recognised him, Mercer 'changed colour very much'. They asked to inspect his cabin and Feast requested him to produce the clothes he was wearing on Saturday. Mercer took out a long bag full of clothes in which O'Grady soon found a pair of bloodstained trousers. Near the bottom of the bag he discovered the cap, scarf and coat that Mercer had been wearing. There was blood on the scarf, and the left cuff of the coat was also soaked. O'Grady noticed that Mercer's socks were full of gorse prickles. When questioned about the blood Mercer said, as he had told Russell and Hall, that he had been killing a sheep. When asked to produce the knife he said he never carried one. When Feast enquired how he cut up his tobacco Mercer replied that he did it with the galley knife. (He was the ship's cook.) When confronted about the large scratch on his nose he claimed he got it on board the *Canterbury*.

O'Grady then took Mercer in charge and told him to come ashore. At the police station Mercer was asked to undress, and O'Grady called Feast's attention to the large number of gorse prickles on his legs and knees. Mercer denied that they were prickles, and defied the policemen to get them out. O'Grady then sent for Dr Rouse, who came equipped with tweezers and extracted a number of gorse prickles from Mercer's hands, fingers, thighs and knees. These were kept to be compared with the prickles that had been noticed on the victim's legs. Later that morning Dr Rouse and Dr Hugh Macdonald conducted a post-mortem examination of Isabella Thompson's body.

There was a large crowd of people both inside and outside Lyttelton's Mitre Hotel that afternoon when the inquest was held before the coroner, Dr Coward. The jury was told that a man named John Mercer had been charged with the murder and remained in custody. All the above witnesses, except the boys, identified Mercer as the man they had seen that Saturday. The foreman of the jury asked to hear some evidence read out again, and once that was done Dr Coward said that was all the evidence for the Crown. Mercer had asked for a solicitor and been advised to say nothing. The room was cleared, and the jury deliberated for only a few minutes before returning a verdict of wilful murder. Mercer appeared in the Magistrate's Court a few days later and was committed for trial in the Christchurch Supreme Court.

By the time the trial opened before Mr Justice Williams on 9 April 1875 there was intense public interest in the case, and a host of people had assembled outside the courthouse long before its doors were due to open. Dr Back, the sheriff, had taken precautions to prevent any unseemly scramble for seats, and there was no confusion or disturbance as the police controlled the entry of the crowd into the public gallery. The reporter for the *Lyttelton Times* thought the prisoner was extraordinarily calm and self-possessed, gazing around the court 'with a degree of *sang froid* that was quite at variance with the serious nature of the charge on which he was indicted'. He seemed an ordinary-looking man 'of the artisan class', and a physiognomist would need to have 'wonderful powers of discrimination' to single him out as a murderer. Mercer pleaded not guilty. He was defended by Thomas Joynt, and Thomas Duncan, as usual, was the Crown prosecutor.

The mate of the *Canterbury*, James Allen, recounted, as he had for the inquest, how he had been in Lyttelton with his skipper, Captain

John Russell, and they had first seen Mercer about 2pm. They saw him again from the corner by the Albion Hotel about 5.10pm. He was coming up Canterbury Street and was walking with a little girl. They crossed the road and Mercer said something to Captain Russell about his wages:

> The little girl went up the street towards Scott's public-house, and Mercer followed her ... She had on a white straw hat trimmed with dark and light ribbons ... I saw Mercer join the little girl up the street, and hang down his head as if he were talking to her ... I can swear that her clothes were clean ... They walked up the street side by side ... I went down the street the other way.

Captain Russell confirmed all of Allen's testimony, adding that they never had occasion to kill any sheep on board the ship: all of their meat was delivered already dressed. He told the court a great deal about the other members of the crew, some of whom were not exactly friends with John Mercer. He said he had asked Allen if he knew who the girl was, 'because Mercer had attempted the very same thing on a little girl, nine years old, at the Buller'. Defence counsel Thomas Joynt objected to any further questioning on this matter, and Mr Justice Williams ruled in his favour.

Nathan Percy repeated his previous damning evidence about his conversation with Mercer, in which he spoke of getting a girl and threatening to cut her throat 'or her weasand' if she refused to co-operate. After the court heard from other witnesses who had given evidence at the inquest, the court was adjourned, and the jurors were taken to a hotel, where they were guarded overnight by two constables.

When the trial resumed at 10 o'clock the next morning Mercer appeared as calm and self-possessed as he had at the start. Sergeant-Major O'Grady and Detective Feast now gave their evidence, adding details that had not been heard at the inquest. Feast admitted that after they had found the bloodstained clothing in Mercer's cabin, and had remarked on the skin missing from his nose, he had blurted out, 'You murdered that poor girl; that is the mark of her fingers – the brand of Cain on your nose!' Mercer had muttered something to the effect, 'Would you like me to say I did it?', but said no more. O'Grady's recollection was that he had said, 'Would you like me to admit it?' Mercer said he had scraped his nose on the *Canterbury*, but there were scratches on his hands as well. Mercer had admitted that the trousers, coat and French 'cheese-cutter' cap were the ones he had worn on Saturday.

Feast said he had first seen the victim's body at the Lyttelton police station at 6.30pm on the Saturday. The Crown prosecutor called for the victim's clothing to be produced, at which 'a thrill of horror ran through the Court at the soiled and tattered appearance which they presented'.

When cross-examined by defence counsel, Feast admitted that another man had been arrested on the Sunday, after identification by one of the boys who had found the body. But as a result of information received he had gone out to the *Cleopatra* with Sergeant-Major O'Grady and arrested Mercer and the other man was released: 'The style of his beard and the coat he was wearing were similar.' The boy had said, 'That is like the man,' but he was very young and had clearly been mistaken. Another suspect had been taken to the police yard in Christchurch, but after examining his clothes, knees and legs Feast was satisfied he could not be the man they were seeking. This suspect had paid his own fare to come to Lyttelton and make a statement, establishing his alibi.

When Dr Rouse described the victim's body and the wound on her neck there were gasps of horror from the public gallery. He thought that death would have been almost instantaneous after the severing of the carotid artery. The court then heard detailed evidence about the microscopic examination of the prickles taken from Mercer, and from the victim's body. They were all gorse prickles.

In his final address to the jury the Crown prosecutor described the case as a 'murder of no ordinary nature'. It had been committed in broad daylight, close to houses and a public street. It was a murder committed by a strong man upon a weak and defenceless young girl, and there was no apparent motive, other than the malice of a foul and diabolical murderer. He considered that very little argument was needed on his part to convince the jury of Mercer's guilt, and there was not even a ray of hope for the defence.

Joynt began his address for the defence by saying he hoped nobody would think he wanted to minimise the enormity of the crime that had been committed, 'a crime of the very foulest and brutal nature that could possibly be perpetrated', but he had no doubt that the jury wanted to arrive at the truth, and he would therefore do his duty in referring them to some parts of the evidence that he thought were not conclusive. There were several discrepancies as to timing, but he would not quibble over minutes. The evidence as to the knife was not conclusive, as it was a very common type, and witnesses' descriptions of clothing sometimes differed from the clothing produced in court. He warned the jury that the mate, James Allen, had given his evidence with a good deal of animus against the prisoner, and could not be looked on as an impartial witness. Joynt was surprised that the boy who had identified a different man, who had been arrested on the Sunday after the murder, had not been called to give a positive identification of the accused. Nor were the identifications of Annie Rouse or Susannah Toomey conclusive.

Joynt thought Nathan Percy's dramatic allegation utterly and grossly absurd, because nobody actually intending to grab a girl and cut her throat would tell someone about it beforehand. Mercer may have been drinking that afternoon, but the men he met on the train did not think he was drunk.

Joynt ended by reminding the jury that a man's life was in their hands, and that although he did not want to intimidate or terrify them, the weight of Mercer's blood would be at their doors if his life were wrongfully forfeited. He trusted that they would give their verdict in all sincerity and truth: 'The monster who could have committed such a crime as this is not safe to have in society; he ought to suffer death.' But they must be satisfied '**beyond all reasonable doubt that it was the hand of the prisoner at the bar, and his hand alone, that committed the deed**'.

Mr Justice Williams then reviewed the evidence and concluded with the warning that the evidence was all circumstantial. Indeed, he almost echoed Joynt's own words about reasonable doubt. The jury retired, and returned again after only 12 minutes. The *Lyttelton Times* reporter observed that '[t]here was then intense commotion in Court'. The foreman pronounced a verdict of guilty.

When the registrar asked the accused if he had anything to say, Mercer replied in a firm voice that he was not guilty, even if 50 jurymen said he was: 'I never killed that child.' Mr Justice Williams then told Mercer that since he had shown no mercy to his victim in this brutal murder, he must expect no mercy from the society he had outraged. He then donned the black cap and sentenced Mercer to death by hanging.

The police took Mercer out by a side door into a waiting cab, while another carriage waited at the main door. They wanted no repetition of the ugly mob that had pursued Cedeno from the court-house four years earlier. On the train to Lyttelton Mercer smoked his pipe and seemed entirely unconcerned about his fate. One reporter noticed with horror that he 'now and then beat time with his feet as if to a tune'. At Lyttelton, however, hundreds of people had gathered to jeer and hoot at him as he was taken up Oxford Street to the gaol.

A month later, on 8 May 1875, he became the third man to be executed at the Lyttelton Gaol, only a few hundred yards away from the gorse hedge where poor Isabella Thompson had bled to death. His death may have satisfied society's demand for retribution, but that was small comfort for the grieving Thompson family.

In 1875 James and Janet McKinlay were living in Chester Street East, near the East Town Belt (now Fitzgerald Avenue), with their four children, aged 13, nine, five and three; another child was on the way. They had moved there about three years before, and neighbours described Janet McKinlay then as 'a clean woman and a good mother'. But her husband had a drinking problem and was prone to violence. Not long after the baby was born he brutally assaulted his wife, and on 12 April was sentenced to three months in prison with hard labour. How was Janet McKinlay to feed her children with the breadwinner in gaol? At the Magistrate's Court, after sentencing, James McKinlay told her to apply for some money due to him as wages, and this she did, receiving £3 10s. Instead of being a comfort, however, the money proved to be a curse.

On Friday 16 April concerned neighbours told the police that they feared the infant had died. Sergeant Henry Kennedy went to the house, where he discovered Janet McKinlay 'on a bed, stupidly drunk'. The baby was lying at her back, dead. Kennedy also found a bottle half full of Irish whiskey, and another, empty.

One of the neighbours, Jane Johnston, told the inquest, held on the Saturday afternoon, that she had met the second son, who had told her his little sister was dead. He also said his mother was 'dead drunk'. She fetched another neighbour, Sarah Carter, and they knocked at the door. When Janet McKinlay appeared they asked her if the baby was dead. She replied 'in a very strange manner' that her daughter had died the day before. Sarah Carter then sent for the police. Jane Johnston told the inquest that the baby had been born a fortnight earlier, and was a weak and sickly infant: 'the child was not a healthy looking one'. She added that Janet McKinlay had been a good mother 'and a sober woman', and had not been drinking at the time of the birth. However, Sarah Carter said that she had seen Janet McKinlay 'the worse for drink' several times since: 'The child was anything but clean, and did not appear as if it had been properly cared for.'

Dr Powell, who had conducted the post-mortem examination, told the inquest that the baby was 'puny and ill-nourished'. There were no external signs of injury, except for a small bruise on the top of the head, and the organs of the body were normal, but apart from a small quantity of milky matter in the stomach, 'the intestines were empty from beginning to end'. He attributed the death to neglect and lack of food. The inquest returned a verdict of manslaughter and committed Janet McKinlay to stand trial at the next sitting of the Supreme Court. That day, too, the McKinlay children, Duncan, Malcolm, John and Jane, were 'brought up under the Neglected Children's Act' and remanded until Monday, when Duncan was sent to the Industrial School for three years and the others for seven years. The school, opened at Burnham in 1874, was intended for neglected or troublesome children.

The key witness at the trial, which opened on 5 July, was Janet McKinlay's eldest son, Duncan. He was 13, though the newspapers described him as a little boy. At the inquest he had said that nobody had attended to the baby on the Wednesday and Thursday, and that his mother had been in bed and sick 'from drinking a lot'. Now he gave this testimony to a hushed courtroom:

> I remember my mother having a little child. I remember the day on which the baby died. I saw it dead in my mother's arms. When I came in at twelve o'clock, my mother was up. She said the baby was dead. She told me not to tell anybody. I told Malcolm, my brother, who is next to me. That night my mother was sitting on a chair in the bedroom. She was not sober ... The day before that she sent me for a bottle of whisky. She was not sober that day. I got five bottles of whisky for my mother that week ... My mother gave Malcolm and me some whisky – not much. My mother consumed all the rest. She was not sober lots of days before the child died ... I am the oldest child. My father was in gaol all the time.

At this point Janet McKinlay asked her son a question, to which he replied: 'On the Saturday night [10 April], my father threw you against the oven door. He put you and the baby out, and would not let you in all night.'

After a short consultation the jury returned a verdict of not guilty and Janet McKinlay was discharged. The newspaper reports stop abruptly at this point, leaving us with many unanswered questions. Who had fed the other children while their mother lay in bed, drunk and incapable? What else had James McKinlay done to his wife, before thrusting her and the baby out that Saturday night?

Had he become angry when he saw that the baby was not being fed properly? Or had he been drinking too? Why had the children not gone to ask for help from the neighbours?

The only clue to the attitude of the neighbours comes from the testimony of Sarah Carter, who told the Supreme Court jury that she had known Janet McKinlay for several years before they came to live nearby, and that she had been a good, sober woman back then, but in recent months she had taken to drink. Sarah had several times seen her drunk before the baby was born, and twice 'beastly drunk' afterwards. When Janet McKinlay told her the baby had died, Sarah had blurted out, 'You bad, wicked woman; I'll send for a policeman, and have you locked up.'

So how did poor Janet McKinlay fare when she returned home? Did the other neighbours help, or shun her as a drunkard who had so neglected her baby that she had died? On 3 April 1876 she was back in the Supreme Court, pleading guilty on a charge of larceny from a dwelling: she had stolen a watch from her employer, Thomas Townsend, in Ferry Road. Mrs Townsend explained that the prisoner had 'come into her service from the hospital, and that up to the period referred to her character had been exceedingly good'. She did not wish to press charges, as she believed that the prisoner had taken the watch 'not with any felonious intent, but to convert it into money for drink, to which unhappily she had latterly become addicted. She would gladly receive her back again, and look after her.' After speaking 'in terms of high eulogium of the kindness of Mrs Townsend', His Honour sentenced Janet McKinlay to be imprisoned until the rising of the court.

This sad little case gives us a glimpse of the desperate conditions in which the poorer people of Christchurch lived in the 1870s, and the dire effects of cheap alcohol on families.

EPILOGUE

We are accustomed to stories that have a beginning, a middle and an end. But history is an unending story, and it is often hard to decide where to stop a particular narrative, unless it concerns a well-defined event, such as a war or an epidemic. This collection of stories, however, seems to have a natural ending in the mid-1870s, for a variety of reasons.

Christchurch and Canterbury were changing, maturing and expanding. From primitive beginnings in 1849, the British colony promoted by the Canterbury Association had become established, and had prospered, initially thanks to exports of wool, then, as the Canterbury Plains were subdivided and cultivated, to a bonanza of wheat exports in the 1870s. The basic infrastructure of roads, bridges and railways was in place, and Christchurch had grown from a straggling village of wooden shops and cottages to become a nascent Victorian city, with handsome public buildings and tree-lined parks, and a population of nearly 20,000, if Lyttelton was included. It was usually known to the rest of New Zealand as 'the city of the plains', since its enduring identification as 'the cathedral city' was still a little way off: the Anglican cathedral was not completed until 1881.

Canterbury had enjoyed over 20 years of virtual self-government under the provincial system, but that was about to change. Its regime had been one of the most successful in the country, investing its revenue from land sales and customs duties in essential projects, but other provinces, especially those in the North Island, had struggled with limited income and major disruptions from the land wars of the 1860s. A campaign to abolish the provincial system gathered strength in the early 1870s and succeeded in 1876, when the central government in Wellington took over the funds (and debts) of the provinces and New Zealand acquired the centralised unitary government it has enjoyed (or endured) ever since. Many things were reorganised after 1876, including the administration of prisons, hospitals, harbours and the railways. Christchurch's courts and prisons became part of a national system, controlled from the capital. These changes set the period 1850–75 in perspective as part of the founding phase of New Zealand's society and government.

There were also changes in key personnel that make the mid-1870s a convenient place at which to end this collection of Christchurch crimes and scandals.

The city's resident magistrate since 1864, Christopher Bowen, had been invited to take a seat on the Legislative Council and to join the cabinet of the central government as minister of justice. He welcomed the move, and when critics muttered that he was a civil servant promoted to political office he stood for the Kaiapoi seat in the House of Representatives, and won it in January 1875. At his last magistrate's sitting, on 3 December 1874, the entire Canterbury legal fraternity turned out to wish him well, and Thomas Duncan, as president of the Canterbury Law Society, thanked him for 'the able and kindly manner' in which he had discharged his duties, adding that in appointing him justice minister the government had got 'the right man in the right place'.

Bowen, who remained the member for Kaiapoi until 1881, had disliked the provincial system, and keenly supported the expansionist policies of the Vogel and Atkinson administrations between 1874 and 1877. In his ministerial role he was not a reformer but he introduced the 'mark system' for good behaviour in the gaols, and as an experienced former magistrate kept a paternal eye on the justice system. His only legislative achievement was the Debtors and Creditors Bill of 1876.

As Peter Lineham remarks in the *Dictionary of New Zealand Biography*, Bowen's greatest interest was in education. He had chaired the Canterbury Education Board in 1873–74 and was president of the Collegiate Union, which set up Canterbury College in 1873 as an affiliate college of the new University of New Zealand. He was probably largely responsible for the Education Act of 1877, which gave New Zealand its much-admired system of free, compulsory, secular state education. After his retirement from politics he returned to Christchurch and became a director of two leading loan companies and the New Zealand Shipping Company. He was made a life member of the Legislative Council and became its Speaker in 1905, ending his career with a knighthood in 1910 and the KCMG in 1914.[1]

Henry Gresson announced his retirement from the bench a little over a year after Bowen's, on 4 February 1875. A parliamentary committee in 1874 had recommended a change in the arrangement of the judiciary that would have seen him moved to Nelson. Gresson, now aged 66, had settled in Christchurch and did not want to move. Like his brother judges he considered this proposal an interference with the independence of the judiciary, and objected to being moved about the country at the whim of politicians. So he chose to resign.

He had already invested in a farm at Woodend, 25km north of Christchurch, and built a comfortable residence there which he named Waiora. He now became something like the local squire of Woodend, giving money towards the building of a parsonage, and indulged to the full his passion for gardening and farming. Though his house no longer exists, many of the English trees he planted survived to maturity. He became, with Bishop Henry Harper, a driving force in the campaign to build Christchurch's cathedral, and was active in the Anglican Church at both parish and diocesan levels, at one time serving as chancellor for the Canterbury Diocese.

His only son, John Beatty Gresson, followed him into the law, and was admitted to the bar by his father in 1873. But John Gresson committed suicide in 1891 – he threw himself under a train – owing unsecured creditors £20,000. Though the son also owed his father £23,000, Gresson, now the Honourable Mr Justice Gresson, made no claim on the estate, and ensured that all those out of pocket were repaid in full. He had to sell his farm and stock and move back to Christchurch, where he died in Fendalton in 1901 at the age of 89.[2]

Most of the other people named in this book died in obscurity, having faded from the public record after their brief appearances in court, or having served their sentences. Doubtless some could be traced with patient genealogical research, but it is a safe assumption that many, if not all, lived quiet and unremarkable lives, as most ordinary people do, only to be forgotten as their grandchildren died.

While some people will always be rule-breakers and trouble-makers, at least for some part of their lives, most of society does its best to stay on the right side of the law and to keep out of the courts. The dishonest are usually found out, as we still see today in high-profile cases of corporate fraud or insider trading. Human institutions continue to operate largely on trust, and it is natural for us to feel disgust for those individuals caught siphoning the funds of hospital boards or charities into their own pockets, and to think that their sentences are far too light.

We live in an age where crimes of violence are all too common, especially those perpetrated against children, and even defenceless babies. All too often such offences are fuelled by alcohol or drugs, or both. No wonder our forebears in the late nineteenth century attempted to secure the prohibition of alcohol. As we have seen in many of the cases described in this book, excessive consumption of alcohol was a major contributor to crime back then. It still is today. Yet prohibition, when it was tried in the United States, only created other evils, and was finally abandoned.

Today we face a much more pervasive and intractable threat to our persons and property from crimes committed by individuals addicted to powerful drugs such as heroin or P (methamphetamine). In order to feed their habit, addicts are compelled to steal and to become pushers, so that they can increase their illicit income. Christchurch families are still being torn apart by their teenagers' addictions to drink and drugs, even as the city struggles to recover from the 2010 and 2011 earthquakes. Police cells at the weekends are crowded with teenage offenders, some of whom are openly boastful in their defiance of the law and the rest of respectable society.

When media pundits and politicians call for harsher sentences, perhaps we should remember that the much harsher prison system of the nineteenth century failed to prevent crime, and in some cases only turned accidental offenders into hardened career criminals. Prison conditions have improved enormously since then, to the point where the taxpayer must wonder if things have been made too comfortable for society's wrongdoers. It has been said that about half the inmates of New Zealand's prisons suffer from some sort of mental illness. The other half might well blame unhappy or deprived childhoods for all their bad life choices. Poverty, mental illness, social isolation, poor education and unemployment are still the root causes of crime, just as they were in the nineteenth century. Until such time as we do something effective about these chronic social problems, our prisons will continue to be overcrowded breeding grounds for yet more crime.

ENDNOTES

Chapter One: Godley Deals with the Ungodly

1. C. E. Carrington, *John Robert Godley of Canterbury*, Whitcombe & Tombs, Christ-church, 1950, pp. 135–36.
2. Gerald Hensley, 'Godley, John Robert', from the *Dictionary of New Zealand Biography*: www.TeAra.govt.nz/en/biographies/1g12/1
3. For a series of informative essays on Godley, see Mark Stocker (ed.), *Remembering Godley*, Hazard Press, Christchurch, 2001.

Chapter Two: Run, Ronage, Run!

1. 'Non-suited' means that the plaintiff voluntarily withdraws a legal action, or the judge decides that the plaintiff has failed to make out a legal course of action, or has brought insufficient evidence to justify the action.
2. Madeleine Seager, *Edward William Seager*, Heritage Press, Waikanae, 1987, pp. 33–35.
3. O. T. J. Alpers (ed.), *The Jubilee Book of Canterbury Rhymes*, Whitcombe & Tombs, Christchurch, 1900, p. 16.

Chapter Three: The Riccarton Poisoning of 1859

1. *Lyttelton Times*, 15 October 1859.

Chapter Four: The Brothel-keeping Policeman

1. Barry Thomson and Robert Neilson, *Sharing the Challenge: A social and pictorial history of the Christchurch police district*, Caxton Press, Christchurch, 1989, pp. 37–38, 269.
2. David Green, 'Cash, Martin', from the *Dictionary of New Zealand Biography*: www. TeAra.govt.nz/en/biographies/1c9/1
3. Thomson and Neilson, p. 37.

Chapter Ten: The London Restaurant Fire of 1870

1. Gordon Ogilvie, *Ballantynes: The story of Dunstable House 1854–2004*, J. Ballantyne & Co., Christchurch, 2004, pp. 18–19.
2. *Lyttelton Times*, 5 September 1907.

Epilogue

1. Peter J. Lineham, 'Bowen, Charles Christopher', from the *Dictionary of New Zealand Biography*: www.TeAra.govt.nz/en/biographies/1b26/1
2. Canterbury Museum, Macdonald Dictionary of Canterbury Biographies, G 429.

Index